Thoreau's Legacy

A Project of the Union of Concerned Scientists and Penguin Classics

American Stories about Global Warming

With a Foreword by Barbara Kingsolver

Richard Hayes, editor

Union of Concerned Scientists • Penguin Classics
CAMBRIDGE, MASSACHUSETTS 2009

LIBRARY OF CONGRESS CATALOGING-IN-PUBLICATION DATA
Thoreau's legacy : American stories about global warming / Richard Hayes, editor ;
foreword by Barbara Kingsolver.
    p. cm.
 ISBN-13: 978-0-938987-06-2 (hardcover)
 ISBN-10: 0-938987-06-2 (hardcover)
1. Global warming—Anecdotes. 2. Philosophy of nature. 3. Human ecology.
4. Thoreau, Henry David, 1817–1862. I. Hayes, Richard, 1968-
 QC981.8.G56T54 2009
 363.738´74—dc22   2009020646

The views expressed in this volume are those of the individual authors.

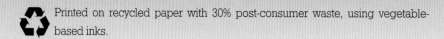 Printed on recycled paper with 30% post-consumer waste, using vegetable-
based inks.

Book design by Sabrina Bowers of Penguin Classics. Portland Tram photo © 2009
Gary Braasch. Daniel T. Blumstein photo courtesy of UCLA. Randall Curren photo
courtesy of Glenna Curren.

This anthology is dedicated to the **millions of Americans taking action** to solve global warming.

Contents

I   Treasured Places, Shifting Seasons

II   Water and Ice

VI Faith and Convictions

VII For Tomorrow

Foreword:
Day Seventy-nine

Barbara Kingsolver

WE FIND OURSELVES IN A CHAPTER OF HISTORY
I would entitle "Isolation and Efficiency, and How They Came Around to Bite Us in the Backside." We're ravaged by disagreements, bizarrely globalized, with the extravagant excesses of one culture washing up as famine or flood on the shores of another. Even the architecture of our planet—climate, oceans, migratory paths, things we believed were independent of human affairs—is collapsing under the weight of our efficient productivity. Twenty years ago, climate scientists first told Congress that carbon emissions were building toward a disastrous instability. Congress said, We need to think about that. Ten years later, the world's nations wrote the Kyoto Protocol, a set of legally binding controls on our carbon emissions. The United States said, We still need to think about it. Now we watch as glaciers disappear, the lights of biodiversity go out, the oceans reverse their ancient order. A few degrees look so small on the thermometer. We are so good at measuring things and declaring them under control. How could our weather turn murderous, pummel our coasts, push new diseases like dengue fever onto our doorstep? It's an emergency on a scale we've never known, and we've responded by following the rules we know: efficiency, isolation. We can't slow productivity and consumption—that's unthinkable. Can't we just go home and put a really big lock on the door?

Not this time. Our paradigm has met its match. Now we can either shift away from a carbon-based economy or find another place to live. Imagine it: we raised our children on a lie. We gave them this world and promised they could keep it running on *a fossil substance*—dinosaur slime—and it's running out. The geologists disagree only on how much is left, and the climate scientists now say they're sorry, but that's not even the point: we won't have time to use it all. To stabilize the floods and firestorms, we'll have to reduce our carbon emissions by 80 percent within a few decades.

We're still stuck on a strategy of bait and switch: okay, we'll keep the cars but run them on ethanol made from corn! But ... we use petroleum to grow the corn. Even if you like the idea of robbing the food bank to fill the tank, there is a math problem: it takes nearly a gallon (or more, by some accounts) of fossil fuel to render an equivalent gallon of corn gas. Think of Jules Verne's novel in which the hero is racing Around the World in Eighty Days and finds himself, on day seventy-nine, stranded in mid-Atlantic on a steamship that has run out of coal. Phileas Fogg convinces the captain to pull up the decks and throw them into the boiler. "On the next day the masts, rafts, and spars were burned. The crew worked lustily, keeping up the fires. There was a perfect rage for demolition." The captain remarked, "Fogg, you've got something of the Yankee about you." Oh, novelists. They always manage to have the last word, even when they're dead.

How can we get from here to there without burning up our ship? That must be our central task now: to escape the wild rumpus of carbon-fuel dependency in the nick of time. We must make rules that were previously unthinkable, imposing limits on what we use and possess. We must radically reconsider the power relationship between humans and our habitat. In the words of my esteemed colleague and friend Wendell Berry, the new Emancipation Proclamation will not be for a specific race or species, but for life itself. We Americans are the 5 percent of humans who have made around 30 percent of all the greenhouse gases emitted since 1750. But our government has been reluctant to address the issue, for one reason: it might hurt our economy. For a lot of history, many nations said exactly the same thing about abolishing slavery: We can't grant humanity to all people—it would hurt our cotton plantations, our sugar crop, our balance of trade. Until the daughters and sons of a new wisdom declared: We have to find another way. Enough of this shame.

Have we lost that kind of courage? Have we let economic growth become our undisputed master again? As we track the unfolding disruption of natural and global stabilities, young people are told to buy into business as usual: you need a job. Do what we did, preserve a profitable climate for manufacture and consumption at any cost. Even at the cost of the other climate, the one that was hospitable to life as we knew it.

In the awful moment when someone demands at gunpoint, "Your money or your life," the answer is not supposed to be difficult. And in fact a lot of people are rethinking the money answer, looking behind the cash price to see what it costs us to mine and manufacture, to transport, to burn, to bury. What did it harm on its way here? Could I get it closer to home? In previous generations we rarely asked about the hidden costs; we put them on layaway. But the bill has come due. Some European countries are calculating the "climate cost" of consumer goods and adding it to the price. We're examining the moralities of possession, inventing renewable technologies, recovering sustainable food systems. We're even warming up to the idea that the wealthy nations have to help the poorer ones, for the sake of a reconstructed world. Generosity will grind some gears in the machine of Efficiency, but we can retool.

The arc of history is longer than human vision. It bends. We abolished slavery, we granted universal suffrage. We have done hard things before. Each time it took a terrible fight between people who could not imagine changing the rules and those who said, "We already did. We have made the world new." The hardest part will be to convince ourselves of the possibilities and hang on. If we run out of hope at the end of the day, we'll rise in the morning and put it on again with our shoes. Hope is the only reason we won't burn what's left of the ship and go down with it. If somebody says, "Your money or your life," you can say, "Life." And mean it.

Introduction

Elda Rotor and Kevin Knobloch

IN THE FALL OF 2008, PENGUIN CLASSICS AND THE Union of Concerned Scientists, with the help of hundreds of bookstores across the country, called for interested citizens to submit their personal stories about global warming for a new anthology. The response to our call was overwhelming, making clear how global warming is affecting people's lives and the places they cherish, as well as the steps they are taking to address the problem.

The essays we selected represent a variety of perspectives, voices, and experiences. The writers include scientists, students, grandparents, activists, veterans, journalists, evangelical Christians, artists, and businesspeople. Their muses are as diverse as their backgrounds.

The chapters are loosely organized by theme. After this introduction, we decided to let the authors' words speak for themselves. We thought it fitting that the first two essays pay tribute to the namesake of this volume, Henry David Thoreau. Thoreau was a writer of uncommon power and a keen observer and recorder of his environment; he seemed to us to be an appropriate figure to represent a partnership between a science-based nonprofit organization and a publisher of literary classics, for he was, in a sense, a kind of literary scientist.

More than 150 years after the publication of *Walden*, Thoreau still calls us to meditate on our own lives and to pay close attention to the natural world and what we can learn from it. In *Walden* and his other works, Thoreau inspired a long line of great American environmental champions and writers, such as John Muir, Aldo Leopold, and Rachel Carson, who introduced readers to landscapes and their indigenous inhabitants—creatures with as much heroism, villainy, grace, and beauty as the great human characters of classic literature. There are too many outstanding works to note here, but we each have our favorites. For Elda it is Rachel Carson's *Under the Sea-Wind*, with its breathtaking and scenic, humble and majestic observations of the natural world of the air, the land, and the oceans. For Kevin it is Don Schueler's *A Handmade Wilderness*, a moving account of two friends who buy a worn-out piece of land in Mississippi and restore it to beauty, health, and usefulness.

There may be no better current example of Thoreau's legacy than Barbara Kingsolver. Every sentence she writes crackles with energy, and her foreword to this collection is a powerful call to actively combat climate change. Indeed, the science shows that we need to act now if we are to have any hope of stopping the worst consequences of global warming.

Our organizations are proud to bring you this exceptional group of thoughtful and inspiring personal stories about global warming. The authors follow in the long tradition of American environmental writers who have broadened our awareness and sharpened our perspective about the world we share.

They are Thoreau's legacy.

Elda Rotor   **Kevin Knobloch**
Editorial Director   President
Penguin Classics   Union of Concerned Scientists

Treasured Places, Shifting Seasons

I

The Warming of Walden

Michelle Nijhuis

I KNEW CLIMATE CHANGE HAD NO BOUNDARIES; AS a science journalist, I'd seen the fingerprints of global warming in Yosemite and Yellowstone national parks and in the highest peaks of the Rocky Mountains. Even so, I didn't expect to see its effects on the shores of Walden Pond.

One early spring day not long ago, I accompanied the Boston University biologists Abe Miller-Rushing and Richard Primack as they followed Henry Thoreau through the historic sites of Concord, Massachusetts. Thoreau, it turns out, was more than a prolific author, determined iconoclast, and legendary cheapskate: he was also an avid amateur botanist who walked miles in pursuit of the earliest blossoms, collecting specimens in his dilapidated straw hat. "I have the habit of attention to such excess," he once complained, "that my senses get no rest, but suffer from a constant strain."

With Thoreau's detailed botanical records in hand, Miller-Rushing and Primack retraced the philosopher's steps, noting how flowering times have changed since Thoreau roamed the woods a century and a half ago. They took me botanizing through the crowds of tourists at Walden Pond, on the train tracks near the site of Thoreau's cabin, and even on the grassy slopes near his grave.

The scientists told me that, on average, spring flowers in Concord were blooming a full seven days earlier than in the 1850s and that their statistics showed a clear and close relationship between earlier flowering times and rising winter and spring temperatures. Thanks to Thoreau's obsessive data collection—and their own efforts to decipher his crabbed handwriting and match his exploits in the field—

> They took me botanizing through the **crowds of tourists** at Walden Pond...

they'd found that climate change had touched even the mythic American landscape of Concord.

Their discovery doesn't cast much light on the path ahead. "Now that we know what's changing, what are we going to do about it, and what are species going to do on their own about it?" reflected Miller-Rushing. "Those are unanswered questions." But their work does show how deeply climate change has already penetrated our back yards—and how citizens, from the noted to the obscure, can help track its effects.

Primack and Miller-Rushing are still digging for data in unlikely places. They've collected the records of modern-day amateur naturalists and used them to study changes in bird migrations along the East Coast. They recently heard that the owner of Polly's Pancake Parlor in New Hampshire has a three-decade-long record of the timing of fall foliage in the White Mountains. Bit by bit, scribble by scribble, they and their collaborators—living and dead—are assembling a picture of the past and the unsettling future. With each new finding, their most famous associate seems more prescient than ever: "My expectation ripens to discovery," Thoreau wrote in his journal in 1856. "I am prepared for strange things."

Michelle Nijhuis *is an award-winning science journalist and former biologist. She lives off the electrical grid in rural western Colorado with her husband and daughter.*

Skinny-Dipping at Walden

Melissa M. Juchniewicz

FOR MOST AMERICANS, HENRY DAVID THOREAU IS A clear but distant voice. But growing up in Concord, Massachusetts, I had a very different perspective of my ancestral townsman. I picked blueberries in the same woods as Thoreau, wandered the same meadows, played in the same sweet, spring-fed waters of Walden and its sister, White Pond.

About a hundred years after *Walden* was written, Walden Pond had a public swimming beach with a snack bar and, across the street, a trailer park. On the shores of White Pond, which is connected to Walden by deep underground springs, were summer camps; some, like my family's, were winterized and lived in year-round. My neighborhood was on the wrong side of the tracks, although I delighted in hearing the train whistle and running to those tracks to wave to the conductor.

That whistle was one of my favorite sounds. The other was the frogs. I went to sleep on summer nights to the deafening music of the bullfrogs. In April I strained to hear the early peepers, signaling spring. The tree frogs' songs were so unique, I felt that no one else in the world knew them as I did.

My best memories are of the woods and ponds. Walking the paths around the ponds, I would stop every few steps to look closely at a dragonfly, a fish, or a frog. The frogs were invisible until they blinked or hopped into the water, and they didn't mind being petted between the eyes or held cupped in my hands for a closer look. When I was a teenager, my high-spirited friends and I would respond to spring fever by skipping school and following the paths to Walden. There we had the world to ourselves as we skinny-dipped and sunned on the rocks on the north side of the

> I went to sleep on summer nights to the deafening **music of the bullfrogs.**

pond, across from the pile of rocks marking the spot where Thoreau had built his cabin. We heard the train on its way to Boston, the wind in the leaves, and the frogs.

Years later, when I visited my mother at White Pond, I was stunned by the silence. In that whole summer night, I didn't hear a single frog. I miss my private world of woods, meadows, and ponds, which are now something of a theme park for those interested in Concord's history. I don't begrudge sharing my hometown with others, but when I learned what had happened to my frogs, I was horrified.

Walden Pond, once a secret, sacred place. Photo by Melissa M. Juchniewicz.

That delicate skin I used to pet allows the frogs to breathe, but it makes them more vulnerable to pollution, pesticides, and ultraviolet rays than any other group of animals. Scientists consider them an early-warning system: their vulnerable skin and fragile eggs mean that they will die from global warming before other groups. To me, frogs are more than a warning system. They represent the mysterious beauty of nature, the infinite curiosity of childhood, and the discovery of youthful freedom.

The loss of the frogs and what they represent is, to me, a boundless tragedy.

Melissa M. Juchniewicz *worked in the professional theater before becoming a teacher of language and education. She lives with her husband in an 1812 farmhouse in Chester, New Hampshire.*

Black Spring

DURING THE WINTER OF 2006-2007, THE MILD WEATHER in Sewanee, Tennessee, at the southern end of the Cumberland Plateau, made me vaguely uneasy. I told myself that we live in a transition zone, so particular natural events have taken our attention at odd times: the spring of the dogwood blight, the summer of the ringworm epidemic.

In 2006 we were still finding ticks on the dog in November, when tick season should have ended. December, January, and February came and went without real cold, and by March the nights were eerily balmy. The plants had been totting up the warm nights, and many broke bud four weeks earlier than usual. It was a spring without winter. Dogwoods and redbuds bloomed, bumblebees buzzed around wisteria blossoms, jack-in-the-pulpits sent up sturdy jacks. Tender green leaves emerged on the trees and shrubs.

> It was a **spring without winter.** Dogwoods and redbuds bloomed, bumblebees buzzed...

I filled a nectar feeder in anticipation of our first ruby-throated hummingbird, which arrived on April 3.

A few nights later the temperature dropped to 18 degrees. I arose to find the hummingbird nectar a tube of ice, flowers drooping, insects fallen silent. For four nights temperatures were in the teens. I brought in the nectar feeder after dark and set the alarm so I could put it out again before daybreak. I imagined the hummingbird frozen solid, but each day it appeared.

The wildflowers were not so resilient. When temperatures rose above freezing, they turned to black slime. The forest looked as if it had been blowtorched.

Mike and Edie Allen visited us briefly from Riverside, California. Self-described "disaster ecologists," they have studied the effects of hurricanes and volcanoes. They added our crazy spring to their list. Long-term effects? We could only wait and see.

In June we had a new forest canopy, but the trees had to go to the bank and take out a loan to produce it. They could photosynthesize, but fruits and seeds were lost. The summer and fall commenced dry and hot. Lake levels dropped, and water supplies throughout the region were overtaxed. We were in the bull's-eye on the drought map of the Southeast. I watered the brown and dying azaleas with dishwater. The fall of 2007 was a fall without. I swept no acorns from the front walk. No local apples were available. No berries, no rosehips—none. Sparrows looked for a few grass seeds along the roadways. Squirrels and birds used the seed feeders heavily. Millipedes and orb-weaver spiders were nowhere to be found. The deer, small and thin-sided, approached closer than usual and ate every banana peel I tossed out, including the labels.

This year seems "normal," except for several large dead trees in our yard. Plants and animals are making up for last year's triple whammy of heat, freeze, and drought. Hummingbirds have flowers to balance their diet, hollies and dogwoods are loaded with berries, and acorns are beginning to fall. But I look at world temperature trends and realize it may be only a short respite. The unease persists.

Jill Carpenter *has worked as a college biology teacher, used book store owner, science writer, and editor. In her hometown of Sewanee, Tennessee, she helped found the Dead Plants Society, a group of women who meet weekly to draw and share natural history observations.*

Rural Southern Georgia

I NEVER SAW A SPRING SO STORMY. SPRING IS SUPPOSED to be a time of fragrant wisteria and five blue-green eggs the size of jellybeans in a nest box. Spring is mild, emergent, translucent.

It's March. I wake to rain, an army of clouds that darken and lower by the hour. By midmorning the weather radio pops on with an alert: *Tornado watch in surrounding counties.* Outside there's lightning, long and brilliant and vicious, accompanied by its sidekick, thunder, rolling in great booms—bowling balls across an alley. I call my mother, who tells me that she and Daddy will get under the stairs if there's a tornado.

"I have never seen daylight this dark," I say. "This is like night."

Rain is falling so hard the ground has long since given up absorbing it. The water is two inches deep in places. The alert radio alarms: a tornado has touched down in Dublin. *Prepare to take shelter immediately.*

I live in a tinderbox. The house, about eighty years old, is made of heart pine, which is very flammable. Some of the windows come out in your hands when you raise them. In the yard, thirty feet from the back door, an old-growth longleaf pine leans toward the house.

My dad calls back. He wants me to get into the ditch out by the road.

"What if I get sucked up?"

"Get in the culvert," he says.

"And if it floods?"

We hang up because I want to listen for a roar like a train. It's hailing, ice chunks so big you could bag and sell them. The weather radio is calling out all the places where tornadoes have been spotted. *Take cover! Should a tornado touch down you will not have time.*

I put blankets on the floor of the small hallway, next to the freezer. I close all the doors leading to the hall.

Growing up in south Georgia, I never heard of tornadoes in spring. They came in summer and fall. Scientists say that warmer temperatures will favor the severe thunderstorms that give birth to tornadoes, and it's possible that the tornado season could shift to what used to be the colder months. This looks like the climate crisis to me.

I wait a long time, thinking, *We are being taken by storm.* But after a while the sky lightens, and finally the weather robot says that the storms are beyond us, farther east, and our county is no longer under a warning. I can come out.

It's hailing, **ice chunks so big** you could bag and sell them.

Janisse Ray, *an author, activist, and naturalist, lives on a family farm in south Georgia.* Ecology of a Cracker Childhood *is her best-known book.*

God's Glorious Gifts

"FEAST YOUR EYES!" MY FATHER SAID TO ME ONE autumn morning. The sun was at just the right angle to hit the leaves of a burning bush in a lucky man's front yard, making the shrub's already vibrant red leaves glow with autumn fervor.

I have been lucky enough to grow up in New England, where we see such wonderful sights each fall, but I have also been lucky enough to visit my mother's tropical homeland, Puerto Rico, every year. Some people may think that the island's exotic climate and always-warm weather must make it paradise, but I tell you that in New England we have it better. It isn't that P.R. isn't a wonderful place, but here we have more to ogle in our own back yard. The glory of God and Mother Nature is the seasons, and nothing is better than autumn leaves and winter frost. I still love to see my breath and pretend it's dragon fire, breathed gallantly on encroaching knights and cooking them to a crisp while I rest in my snowy lair. Yes, fourteen-year-old teens enjoy making the odd snow fort. Isn't that wonderful?

I still love to **see my breath** and pretend it's dragon fire…

Anything and everything that threatens my autumn and winter glory and frolic would be bad, unnatural, and unwanted. I have read about global warming and its impending effects, and I confess that I don't care if the "demon" behind it is fossil fuel, some screwy temperature cycle, giggling aliens with giant mirrors in space, or even that slightly off guy down the street who gives me odd looks when I walk around the block with my old camera to take black-and-white pictures for my Photography 1 course. I just want whatever or whoever is causing global warming to shove off, and I'm willing to make some sacrifices to help that process. I love my New England seasons with all my heart, and the idea of one long summer or one long winter—whatever it is the scientists have lately been predicting—is enough to make me scream in anger and pain.

So the next time you enjoy our wonderful seasons, experiencing the brightly colored leaves, that wonderful fireplace smell in the streets, and snow angels, I want you to walk over to your thermostat and turn it All the Way Down. Shiver a bit. Curl up in bed and read books about kings, dragons, and knights, and stop every other page to act out the dragon's part with your smoky breath. Hell—catch pneumonia and spend a week in front of the fireplace sniffling with family and friends and know that you wouldn't have a fireplace if it weren't for God, Mother Nature, and the seasons. And then look at the red-hot coals in the fireplace and remember that if there's even a snowball's chance in Hell that you're helping protect the seasons, God's glorious gifts, it's worth it.

Diego Paris *is in the ninth grade and lives in Winchester, Massachusetts. An avid reader, he hopes one day to become a science-fiction novelist.*

Thomas Huntington

A Grandfather's Tale

SOME YEARS AGO, WHEN I WAS WORKING IN GREAT Smoky Mountains National Park, I ran into a fellow who worked for the National Park Service. He had a team of pack horses that regularly provisioned volunteers working for extended periods in remote parts of the park. He was from the foothills of the Smokies on the North Carolina side of the park, where his family had lived for generations.

This man spoke with a classic mountain accent, and he spoke from the experience of generations living in an area attuned to the natural world. As we talked about some of the ongoing changes in the forest, he related an anecdote that I will never forget. He told me that his grandfather had said to him, "Time was a man could kill a hog by Thanksgiving, and now a man cain't hardly kill a hog."

He explained that his people had lived back in the hills long before there was electricity for refrigeration, and no one had an ice house, as people did in northern New England. However, up in the cool, damp, shady mountain hollows, meat could be cured without spoiling if the animal was slaughtered late enough in the year; it would remain cool until it was time to cook the meat.

> For a long time **their family tradition** had been to slaughter a hog at Thanksgiving…

For a long time their family tradition had been to slaughter a hog at Thanksgiving and then cure it until Christmas or New Year's in one of those shady hollows. But his grandfather was saying that by the 1980s the climate had warmed so much that it was no longer possible to slaughter a hog with confidence that it would cure without spoiling. Too often a warm spell would arrive and spoil the meat.

As I walk through my woodlot in Maine these days, this story haunts me, and I think about the changes going on around me. Will I be telling my grandchildren about the "olden days," when trees cut from this woodlot warmed us in the cold snowy winters? Will the sturdy fabric of New England, like that of the North Carolina mountains, pass into memories and folk tales?

Thomas Huntington, *a scientist studying the impacts of climate change, lives in Augusta, Maine. He conducted research on acid deposition in the Smoky Mountains in the 1990s.*

Michelle Cacho-Negrete

Last Winter

LATE WINTER BROUGHT FOUR BLIZZARDS NEARLY back to back. Snow is vital to the ecology of Maine, a blanket that insulates the life germinating underground, a womblike protection, very welcome despite treacherous roads, power outages, and "cabin fever." A few weeks earlier I'd been fearful that we would have little snow on the ground, as had happened a year or so before, leaving our flower and vegetable gardens nearly barren. Indeed, just the previous week, 55-degree temperatures had broken weather records, arousing my fears. My husband, Kevin, a research scientist whose work involves trees and global climate change, paused to examine some prematurely budding pussy willows, those furry precursors of spring.

"Nearly two months early," he said, running his fingers over the buds.

The willows were not alone in their confusion as to the season: oak and maple buds had begun to swell, and the sharp tips of daffodils poked out between layers of icy slush. Ice melted from the roof, a sparkling mini-waterfall. The snow on the driveway parted like a wintry Red Sea. The conifers seemed to suck up green from the air. Black dots, stark against the hard-packed snow, came to life: snow fleas, tiny insects beckoned from their dormancy by the April-like weather, frolicked wildly, offering a springtime dance of little hops. Meteorologists spoke about unseasonable cold in some places, unseasonable heat elsewhere, droughts, monsoons, mudslides.

The willows were not alone in their confusion as to the season…

Snow fell again, slicing through the air like thorns, burying the springtails, walling roads with six-foot drifts. Freezing temperatures coated buds in latticed ice, rendering them useless for the spring to come, reminding me again how fragile and yet resilient everything is and how carelessly we challenge that resilience.

I curled up by our wood stove and read a book about Inuit shamans on mystical journeys who take on the responsibility of atoning for tribal transgressions and restoring balance to the everyday world. I thought of how our children and grandchildren will be the ones forced to take on that responsibility, apologizing to the planet for the ways we've mistreated it.

Michelle Cacho-Negrete
is a retired psychotherapist who now works as a writer. She lives in Wells, Maine, with her husband.

Marian Wineman

Sugar Shacks, Snow Cones, and Sugar Maples

THE SUGAR SHACK. My sister's school in Hillsboro, New Hampshire, was across a dirt road from a dairy farm of rolling hills and steely gray granite boulders. Just inside the farm's meandering stone walls was an old sugar shack. The dark wood structure, about ten by twelve feet, had multipaned windows and a chimney that looked like a miniature sugar shack atop the steep metal roof.

One day we were shown around the sugar house, with its creaking wooden floorboards. The air inside was so thick, hot, and heavy with sweet vapor that it was nearly intolerable. Wood smoke mingled with the steam. Boiling liquid slowly migrated along a series of sloping interconnected troughs around the perimeter of the shack. We were treated to a taste from each stage of the sugaring-off. The first troughs held a watery, nearly clear liquid. Progressing on down the troughs, the syrup became gradually thicker and darker, its taste increasingly complex.

SNOW CONES. Every spring my family spent a long ski weekend at the Appalachian Mountain Club's Mount Cardigan lodge in New Hampshire. After an eventful day of skiing the rope tow, our mittens sopping wet and the tow often breaking down, we sat down to a tasty dinner, followed by an amazing treat.

Outside the lodge, a huge black iron kettle hung over a roaring fire. Embers snapped

Embers snapped and **danced upward in the frosty air** toward the stark stars overhead.

and danced upward in the frosty air toward the stark stars overhead. Sweet steam boiled up from the cauldron, obscuring the faces of the others stamping their feet in the snow.

Someone handed me a cup, which I carefully filled to the brim with snow, then timidly tiptoed close to the kettle. Using a big ladle, another person poured thick, steamy dark syrup into my snow-filled cup. A maple snow cone!

My mom and little brother catching the rope tow at Cardigan, April 1965. Photo by my dad, Robert J. Wineman.

SUGAR MAPLES. In recent years sugar maples, the source of maple syrup, have been tapped as early as January instead of in March, the traditional time. As winters warm and spring comes earlier, the perfect sap-producing combination of freezing temperatures at night and thawing during the day occurs on fewer days, and maple syrup production wanes.

As a result of these warming trends, the sugar maples' unique growing conditions may no longer occur in New England, and the trees may die out. Soon maple syrup may not be produced at all in New England, only in Canada. How can I tell my daughter and grandchildren that we let the iconic sugar maples disappear?

Marian Wineman *is an environmental consultant living in Seattle with her husband, their nine-year-old daughter, a hamster, fish, and two cats.*

Water and Ice

Danna Staaf

The Unfathomable in Flux

LOS ANGELES IS NOT PARTICULARLY FAMOUS FOR natural beauty, and it is not a coastal city. However, as a child growing up in this urban setting, I was a determined naturalist, and my strongest passion was reserved for creatures of the sea, as portrayed in books and documentaries. Anxious to get a closer look, I decided at the age of twelve to become a scuba diver. Not only did my parents encourage this peculiar ambition, my father enrolled in the scuba course with me.

Our first dives were on Catalina Island, and I recall vividly the thrill of those early underwater experiences. I once turned my head to find myself gazing into the brown, curious face of a harbor seal, mere inches away. I believe I stopped breathing. We regarded each other for one long moment before the creature swam away, leaving me thoroughly enchanted. On another dive I stumbled into a grove of giant kelp. Bright summer sunlight pierced the water in distinct beams, lighting each kelp blade in dazzling yellows, blues, and greens. Distinctive orange garibaldi, California's state fish, swam through the majestic swaying algae, entirely unconcerned by my presence.

> We regarded each other for **one long moment** before the creature swam away...

Now I live in coastal Monterey, a six-hour drive north of Los Angeles, and I can dive almost in my back yard. The sea here is still full of kelp forests, but different animals swim through the fronds. Garibaldi are rare; instead I find monkeyface eels lurking beneath the kelp, their eyes and big lips full of expression. A faunal shift occurs at Point Conception, between Los Angeles and Monterey. To the south are warm-water species; to the north, cold-water. Some animals, like the frolicking harbor seals, are at home in either province, but many others must live on one side or the other.

At least, that was once the case. Now more and more southern species are creeping up around the point, displacing northern species. As stories of expanding and contracting ranges become more common, I struggle with the picture of what my beloved California coast will look like in fifty or a hundred years.

Thoreau wrote, "The ocean is a wilderness reaching round the globe, wilder than a Bengal jungle, and fuller of monsters." In his time the sea was perceived to be a place that human activity could not touch or transform, an endless natural resource, "equally wild and unfathomable." Today, to our sorrow, we find that the ocean is more fragile than we thought. Overfishing has vastly depleted, sometimes extinguished, the awe-inspiring "monsters" of the sea. Global warming is causing sea levels and sea-surface temperatures to rise inexorably, shifting species' ranges and endangering those that fail to adapt.

I love the beauty, diversity, and abundance of the California ocean. I wonder how it will weather the global changes already under way. Will Monterey look more like Catalina when my children learn to dive?

Danna Staaf *is a Ph.D. student at Stanford University's Hopkins Marine Station, in Pacific Grove, California. Her dissertation research is on the development and dispersal of the Humboldt squid.*

Susan Carol Stein

For the Love of Alaskan Ice

EVERYONE SHOULD LICK A GLACIER. IT TASTES A little bit like dinosaurs and looks a little bit like God, whatever that is. Take a good, long lick. You are just one person meaning no harm.

Everyone should hug a glacier with bare hands spread wide. Go on, do it. Run up to it with your arms open, as if it were your favorite grandma. Push your hands into the ice. Feel the old, old cold pulling away even as you make contact. It's not your imagination. The loss is subtle but sincere. Stare at the thin line of black rock between your boots and the glacier's edge. No one has seen that sliver of earth before this moment. No one. It's been buried, protected, unexamined. You begin to feel responsible for exposing the hidden skull of the planet.

Everyone should **hug a glacier** with bare hands spread wide.

How could you know, living all your life in the bellies of cities, that you would fall in love with Alaskan ice? This beautiful blueberry Slurpee that stretches across the top of the earth is changing you.

You learn the size of your carbon footprint and begin to minimize it. You telecommute as often as possible, walk wherever you can. You grow your own organic veggies, buy local, and avoid franchised food. You plant trees and flowers that attract bees and birds. You notice that wildlife now throngs to your healthy back yard, your tiny spot of earth. You use earth-friendly cleaning products and you recycle. You cut plastic out of your life whenever possible. You share your bath with someone special. Conservation is loads more fun than you ever imagined.

You put on another sweater and lower your thermostat. You join the Sierra Club. You pay close attention to what businesses, scientists, and politicians are doing to shift gears, lower the heat, slow down the melt, take full responsibility, and protect what is left. It's time.

Don't feel guilty. Don't blame anyone or blow hot air—we don't need more of that. And don't be overwhelmed, don't panic. These are all petty indulgences. Rather, hold the image of a healthy glacier in your heart and the taste of ancient ice on your tongue. It will change you and gently lead you to make change.

The author at Exit Glacier, Kenai Fjords National Park, Alaska. Photo by Jackie Stratton.

Susan Carol Stein *owns a fair-trade Internet business that donates its net profits to global organizations that aid women and children. She lives in Seattle, where she also volunteers to protect indigenous land in Siberia.*

Edward C. Brainard II

Through a Sailor's Eyes

AS A SAILOR, I VIEW THE WORLD FROM THE SEA, gaining a perspective often lost on land. I feel very close to the sea, where life was created, for my blood runs deep with the balance of its salts.

I have made many Atlantic crossings in small yachts and have seen many storms. You learn to be prepared, to make sure that your yacht is well founded. At the mercy of nature, you develop a profound respect for her power. You are in her realm, and after each storm you are thankful to have survived. You have been given another chance, and deep inside yourself you promise to show her respect and a willingness to give back all she has done for you.

Many wonderful memories come to me. During a dark, foggy night I saw the phosphorescent trails of a mother dolphin and her baby flowing abeam without effort, ribbons of undulating fire. In the morning the two dolphins were still there. They seemed content to be at our side. We developed a fondness for this marvel, a feeling of closeness and respect, a bond that they would be safe in the future.

In 1986 I was planning my first double-handed transatlantic OSTAR race with the help of a meteorologist. We were deciding on a route from Plymouth, England, to Newport, Rhode Island, for the next summer. Normally we see Mercator projections as viewed from the equator, but I spotted one projection looking down from the North Pole. Like magic, I could see three very large storms equally spaced around the globe above the mid-latitudes. The system looked like the planetary gear in an automobile. That one image suddenly made me realize that a storm is not just an isolated

> You are **in her realm,** and after each storm you are thankful to have survived.

event, it is part of a marvelous weather machine driven by the heat of the sun. Everything is interrelated.

The surface temperature of the sea is rising, and violent hurricanes are increasing. Higher ocean acidity threatens the development of shells and corals. Sea level is rising. We know we will see major shifts in weather patterns and ocean currents. Although the future is not clear, there will certainly be immense changes that will have profound effects on future generations. There will be major dislocations of human populations and of all life on our planet. There will be no safe haven.

Only the wise use of our environment and resources will ensure that we can continue. Our efforts to adjust to change will strengthen our role as stewards of our planet, helping to preserve this world so that future generations can enjoy seeing the rising sun at sea, with gales to keep us on our guard. A well-prepared yacht has a much better chance of surviving. Using our planet and its resources intelligently will similarly give us all a better chance of survival.

Edward C. Brainard II, *an inventor and retired executive whose previous company makes oceanographic and environmental instruments, lives in Marion, Massachusetts. He is a Corporation Member of the Woods Hole Oceanographic Institution and a member of the Cruising Club of America.*

Bruce Wright

Chukchi Sea Ice-Out

I LIVE IN ALASKA, AND MY CLIMATE-CHANGE RESEARCH projects are devoted to understanding changes in the distribution of harmful algal blooms, paralytic shellfish poisoning, and domoic acid. I also study highly migratory sharks (salmon sharks and great whites). However, in June 2007 I was teaching a 7 Generations environmental education class in Wainwright, an Inupiat village of about 550 people on the Chukchi Sea. Wainwright is a whaling community and is very connected to the sea for both spiritual and physical sustenance.

My classroom was a hall in the community building, about a hundred meters from the beach, but no waves pounded the shoreline because it was sealed in ice. After class I had plenty of daylight to go exploring; in June the sun is up twenty-four hours a day. Two Inupiat boys playing in the sand above the ice-covered sea asked who I was and what I was doing. We quickly became friends and talked about our communities; mine was Wasilla. I asked about the boats and the meat piled on the ice. They said it was shares of whale meat and muktuk (whale skin and fat) that the community elders had not yet picked up, and they convinced me we should go investigate. I brought my pocket knife, and the three of us shared a little bit of muktuk.

During class on my third day in Wainwright, a man opened the door and excitedly said, "The ice is going out! The ice is going out!" Sure enough, half an hour later, while on break, the entire class walked to the beach and saw that the sea ice had retreated miles offshore. I was especially surprised because there was no wind; the ice seemed to be moving by some strong

> ...there was no wind; the ice **seemed to be moving** by some strong unseen force.

unseen force. By the end of class the sea ice was no longer visible; it was at least twenty miles out. So I went to my room to unpack the folding fishing rod that always accompanies me in my travels and returned to the shore of the Chukchi Sea to fish.

After a while an elder came up behind me and silently watched for about five minutes, then asked, "Catch anything?" I waited a minute, then responded, "No." After making five more casts, I asked if there were any fish here. Five minutes went by while the old Eskimo thought of an appropriate response. Finally he said, "Don't know." Then, after another brief wait, "You are the first human being to fish here in June. Ever."

In 2007 the sea ice at Wainwright went out six weeks earlier than had ever been recorded in local knowledge.

Bruce Wright *lives and works in Alaska as a senior scientist for the Aleutian Pribilof Islands Association and executive director of the nonprofit Conservation Science Institute. When not spending time with his family, he enjoys being in the wilderness, where he is regularly close to wolves, bears, and moose.*

Terril L. Shorb

Climate Change and Creature Comforts

IN THE HIGH DESERT OF THE AMERICAN SOUTHWEST, we know what global climate change *sounds* like. It is the sound of many tongues lapping. When we moved to central Arizona seventeen years ago, one appealing feature was the presence of wild javelina, deer, foxes, coyotes, tarantulas, and a rainbow of birds, from scrub jays to roadrunners. We put out a wet welcome mat in the form of a shallow steel pan of water, which was used mostly by birds for bathing. The pan was usually three-quarters full the next morning.

In the past decade, the "pan index" has changed. Our central Arizona highlands typically receive nearly twenty inches of precipitation annually, but in many of the past ten years we have received significantly less. Foothills and grasslands once glittered with natural catch basins year-round; most are now dry. It is possible to wander twenty thousand square miles of central and northern Arizona and scarcely get your boots wet.

> Foothills and grasslands once glittered with natural catch basins year-round; **most are now dry.**

While some pundits wag their tongues to deny that humans are a causative factor in global climate change, the tongues of the wild creatures in our midst lap at our water pan, which now shows up empty most mornings. We put out more pans. By day javelina sip daintily, and dozens of juncos and white-crowned sparrows perch on the rim, bending low to dip thirsty beaks. At night we have seen a white-throated desert pack rat slake its thirst. Desert hares, gray foxes, a coyote, wasps, beetles, and other wild creatures are regular visitors to the pans.

Another visible effect of the prolonged drought is the precarious drop in a local aquifer, drying up springs that once trickled over parched ground across the region. And that brings us back to the tiny oasis in our back yard. We realize that we must offset the water we provide for wildlife by conserving water elsewhere. We have installed low-flush toilets. We consolidate household washing chores. When exotic trees and shrubs planted by previous owners succumbed to drier conditions, we replaced them with native species that provide forage and shelter for native creatures.

One unexpected form of resource conservation is that we drive fewer miles for entertainment or purchase of "things" for the household, because we love to stay home and observe the never-ending drama of local wildlife. There is a direct correlation between our heightened happiness from interacting with nature and the decline in our material consumption.

Conserving water is a small sacrifice compared to the enormous joy of seeing wild creatures slake their thirst at the little steel water holes. Looking out for other-than-human beings in our natural neighborhood is our way of responding positively to global climate change. The presence of these critters is integral to our daily life. Our small act moderates our consuming ways and gives new meaning to the phrase "providing for creature comforts."

Terril L. Shorb *grew up on ranches and farms in the northern Rockies and now teaches at Prescott College in Prescott, Arizona. He cofounded and directs the college's Sustainable Community Development Program.*

Calving
Tidewater Glacier

My perceptions as a working artist are strongly influenced by the changing landscape. In the last few years I have tried to capture **the complexity and beauty** of these receding icy giants, visual reminders that we humans must align ourselves with the balance of the natural world.

Trude McDermott *has been a painter and mixed-media artist for the past twenty-five years. She lives with her husband in Coarsegold, California, near Yosemite National Park.*

Opposite page: "Calving Tidewater Glacier," oil on canvas by Trude McDermott.

In Defense of Ice

Carol Ellis

...my friends and I jumped crevasses, glancing **down the yawning cuts** into blue ice.

HAVING BACKPACKED ALL MY LIFE, I AM BOUND TO ice and glaciers over rivers of time. Today I see clearly how global warming threatens them. My connection to Glacier National Park began in the summer of 1966. On my days off from work, I hiked hundreds of miles, past Blackfoot Glacier, up to Sperry Glacier, and over Siyeh Pass with its three glaciers. At Grinnell Glacier my friends and I jumped crevasses, glancing down the yawning cuts into blue ice. We climbed along the bottom edge of a snow field, trying to reach the western slope of Salamander Glacier, which lies cradled in the sheer crest of Mount Gould. The rugged terrain stopped us.

In 1971 my husband and I packed our young daughter along the Continental Divide on the back side of the mountain wall, where we scrambled up the notch to look down on Grinnell. From that elevation the glacier looked grayer than I remembered—perhaps because the sky was overcast, I thought. But in 1987, when we hiked from Swiftcurrent Valley toward Grinnell and Salamander, I was shocked. In twenty-one years Salamander Glacier had visibly shrunk. The tail had atrophied, the neck was strangled, the head was more diminutive, the belly had tucked and flattened up toward the spine. Grinnell had also changed. Its contracted surface area looked dirtier and grayer from the melting that had occurred. Many more rocks lay on the surface, as in the Himalayas today. The National Park Service had cordoned off more areas of instability. Where in 1966 we had hopped crevasses and hiked closer to the Salamander, now visitors walked with a ranger. And in 2000, when I crossed over Gunsight Pass past Blackfoot Glacier, I saw that same kind of assault on the compressed ice of the glacier's core.

If I want to confirm that rising temperatures threaten the glaciers, I can look at the winter ice on Waitts Lake in Washington, where I have a cabin. The omens in the ice are grim. Waitts Lake freezes later and melts earlier, often turning into pools of mush rather than thick, jagged icebergs, as it used to in the 1970s. The warm water in the pools drizzles through the mass of ice and softens it. Forty years ago, as fishing season approached toward the end of April, we'd wonder if the ice would clear. We'd sled or skate our children across the lake in January with no qualms. In February we could still hear the ice whoop as it split to allow more freezing. But by the late '80s the ice was usually gone in March, and by the '90s sometimes sooner. Rarely can the ice bear the weight of walkers or snowmobiles as it used to. Also the lake temperatures have risen; swimming season lasts one month longer than it did in the '70s.

As the winters get shorter and the grasses green earlier, the deer multiply. The blackbirds chortle in the cattails sooner. We entertain more clouds of midges in May. Long V's of Canada geese honk their way south even in December. Both wildlife and humans have changed their patterns.

All life flows with the cycles of water. I fear my grandchildren will not be able to enjoy glaciers in Glacier Park or whooping ice at Waitts Lake. I watch warily as we approach the tipping point for saving glaciers, ice, and life on this blue planet.

Carol Ellis *has taught first grade in Spokane, Washington, for over twenty-five years. She raised her own three children to hike, swim, and skate at Waitts Lake.*

Disappearing Coral

In 1993 during a Reef Relief Photo Monitoring Survey dive, yellow-band disease was discovered and documented for the first time *(top)*. Coral bleaching is often associated with rising ocean temperatures *(middle)*. **A five-hundred-year-old coral** has died in a single decade *(bottom)*. It would be a shame if the first generation of divers turned out to be the last to see living coral.

Craig Quirolo, *a photographer and artist who founded the environmental group Reef Relief in 1985. He lives in Brooksville, Florida.*

Opposite page: Disappearing coral, Key West, Florida. Photos by Craig Quirolo.

Kristan Hutchison

Change Is in the Air

A FAMILIAR STENCH BLEW ACROSS THE ARCTIC TUNDRA. My three fellow hikers wrinkled their noses while I looked around with uneasy recognition.

In our travels north of the Arctic Circle on a journalism fellowship to learn about research in Alaska, we had smelled little but dry lichen and the occasional plume of diesel and dust from trucks headed to oil fields at Prudhoe Bay. This new odor reeked of grass clippings and coffee grounds rotting in a swamp. I scanned the ground and horizon for its source, expecting to find moist piles of manure and a few heifers chewing their cud.

This was a smell I remembered from my childhood thirty years ago and 2,780 kilometers south, in the cow pastures of our family farm near Seattle. The moist odor carried memories of idyllic summer afternoons, splashing in a creek as cow pies oozed into the mud and crusted in the sun. But here on Alaska's North Slope there were no cows, no alders leaning over lazy streams, no snakes to catch in the grass.

Except for the Brooks Range to the south, the tundra was so flat and empty I could see the curve of the earth as it stretched toward the Arctic Ocean. Caribou and musk ox grazed these lands rather than cattle, but I saw no sign of them. Here the smell of manure was as disconcerting as if one of the bearded scientists had suddenly spoken to me in my mother's voice.

Seeing where the smell originated intensified my unease. As we walked, a crevice appeared a few yards ahead. The top layer was like a green skin protecting the permafrost below. Now, a few weeks into summer, the skin had cracked open, exposing mud and shards of ice. Dinosaur dung, mastodon manure, and other organic mate-

> This new odor reeked of **grass clippings and coffee grounds** rotting in a swamp.

rials that had been trapped in the frozen ground for thousands of years were suddenly exposed to the relentless Arctic sun. The result was just like leaving a freezer door ajar so the food melts and rots. What I smelled was probably hydrogen sulfide gas released from the tundra. Even more disconcerting was what I couldn't smell: the methane and carbon dioxide rising from the melting permafrost into the atmosphere, adding to the layer of gases that cause global warming.

Poised at the edge of the fresh crevice, I could hear a trickle of water coming from the ground below. The ice was melting into a rank river, like the muddy brook I played in as a child, carving a streambed through half a mile of tundra. What had been frozen was now flowing freely to the sea, ready to add to already rising waters.

Over the past several years I had interviewed scientists about climate change and studied their projections. I knew how high the oceans had already risen. I'd seen the shrinking glaciers. But when I saw the tundra cracks of global warming, what I'd known intellectually punched me in the gut. We have opened a door that will be difficult to close again, because it has set off a cycle of its own. Now, whenever I bring home a bag of manure to fertilize my garden, I'm not comforted by childhood memories but alarmed by the whiff of global warming.

Kristan Hutchison *has worked as a reporter and editor for over twenty years, most of that time in Alaska.*

Mark Hixon

Garden of Ghosts

IT HAD BEEN THE MOST BEAUTIFUL OF TROPICAL forests, more a garden really, a rainbow garden of so many colors and shapes and sheer variety of life that it boggled my mind as much as it pleased my senses. The multiple layers of the canopy housed more life—more species—than any other ecological community on earth. And the sheer diversity of growth forms and behaviors and life cycles was overwhelming, regardless of how closely I looked or how far back I stepped to take it all in. The people living nearby thrived on the cornucopia of foods provided by this supremely productive ecosystem. Pharmaceutical corporations discovered dozens of natural chemicals with novel medicinal properties in this forest, including anticancer agents.

I had loved and studied this Eden for a decade, marveling at its incredible diversity while seeking to understand how so many different kinds of creatures could coexist in such density. I learned that it took many species to regulate the abundance of any one species. The amazingly intricate web of interactions lent credence to the idea that complexity begets stability in nature.

I had loved and **studied this Eden** for a decade, marveling at its incredible diversity...

But stability can be tenuous, lasting for millennia and then ending abruptly. This kaleidoscopic potpourri of millions of species, born of millions of years of evolution, was no match for the accelerating rate at which modern humans have been warming the global climate with ceaseless carbon emissions. It happened so suddenly. One day all the trees of this grand garden, many of them hundreds of years old, turned as white as snow. But it had not snowed. Quite the contrary: record temperatures had caused the trees to expel the colorful single-celled organisms living symbiotically within their tissues, rendering all surfaces colorless. Exactly why the mutualism collapsed no one knew for sure, except that extremely warm temperatures were the main culprit. Whatever the exact mechanism, all of the ashen trees soon died. They stood in place for years as pallid ghosts, gradually overgrown and drilled by tiny organisms. Then, storm by storm, the standing corpses crumbled and fell, and with them fell the entire web of life they had supported—the richest of ecosystems reduced to a barren plain of rubble.

These were not trees as we know them on land. This cemetery had been my favorite coral reef, the corals being the trees of the ocean rainforest. The reef was killed by the great coral bleaching of 1998, one of the warmest years worldwide ever recorded by humans. Nearly 10 percent of all the coral reefs in the world died in that single terrible year, as did many more in 2005, perhaps the warmest year on record … so far. The remaining reefs face both increased bleaching and ocean acidification, which dissolves the corals' limestone skeletons as carbon dioxide mixes with seawater and becomes carbonic acid. The rainbow gardens beneath the tropical seas are dying, along with their uncountable goods and services for humans: unparalleled destruction, unseen and unheard, with no end in sight. As a coral-reef scientist, I feel like a caregiver at a cancer hospice.

Mark Hixon, *a professor of marine biology at Oregon State University, has studied coral reefs around the world for thirty years. He enjoys surfing, scuba diving, and beach treks.*

Clamming

When the tide is out, the table is set.
—*Alutiiq saying*

DIGGING CLAMS ON THE COBBLESTONE BEACHES OF Prince William Sound, Alaska, isn't easy. My son and I are out on the exposed beach of a minus tide, flipping over the seaweed-covered rocks and uncovering a scuttling world of tiny crabs, beach lice, and gunnel fish. We look for the oval holes in the black sand that indicate where the clam's siphon emerges. I do the digging while my little boy picks out the butter clams and littlenecks revealed in the widening hole.

As the ridged white shells, some as big as my fist, drop into the bucket, I can almost smell clam chowder simmering on the stove. But a nagging fear is spoiling the moment. For the first time I have to wonder if the clams are contaminated and not safe to eat.

> I do the digging while **my little boy picks out** the butter clams and littlenecks...

The community was hit hard by the 1989 *Exxon Valdez* oil spill. The resulting damage to the ecosystem has been substantial and is still continuing. But oil contamination is not what worries me. My fear is of contracting paralytic shellfish poisoning (PSP), which develops in shellfish that have ingested a toxic form of algae. The saxitoxin, a type of neurotoxin, in PSP-contaminated shellfish is a thousand times more toxic than cyanide.

PSP has been documented in other parts of the state, but the deep, cold waters of Prince William Sound have been historically free of it. However, with global water temperatures rising, researchers believe it may be only a matter of time before toxicity is documented here.

On Alaskan beaches where clams are harvested commercially, the state tests for PSP. But outside of those areas, no testing is done. There have been efforts to produce a test that rural clam diggers could use to determine if PSP is present, but a kit has not yet been certified.

Other types of pathogenic illnesses are appearing in Prince William Sound for the first time. In 2004 an outbreak of gastroenteritis caused by the bacterium *Vibrio parahaemolyticus* made the passengers on a day-tour boat, who ate contaminated oysters from a commercial farm they visited, very uncomfortable for a few days. Tests on shellfish samples taken around the sound showed an uncommonly virulent type of *Vibrio* that had not been previously documented here. Scientists who study invasive species say this may be a sign of new, more severe outbreaks of diseases caused by pathogens.

Chenega Bay has never experienced a "bad clam" episode, but we are now adopting the rule of thumb used in the southeastern United States: harvest shellfish only in the colder months whose names include an *r*.

It is a cool fall evening, and the clams we are digging should be safe. And we know the symptoms of PSP, just in case. Digging clams will never again be a worry-free endeavor, but we aren't going to let that stop us from enjoying the bounty of the sea.

Katherine McLaughlin *is an educator and environmental consultant in Chenega Bay, Alaska, where she lives with her husband and son. She is a native of the Gulf Coast of Florida.*

Open Spaces

III

Chavawn Kelley

A Million and a Half Acres

ONE OF THE FIRST T-SHIRTS I REMEMBER MY HUSBAND wearing was a pale blue Beefy-T he'd worn to a holey mess. Above a crude mountain silhouette leered a mean-faced smiling bug. The message read "Feast your eyes on the Wind Rivers." Shaun loved that shirt because he'd gotten it the year he worked as a backcountry ranger. Only a few were printed, and it was an insider's joke. Who ever heard of the pine bark beetle munching away at the Wind River Range?

I'd always said I wanted to marry a man who loved the mountains as much as I did. We married in a cottonwood grove, and for years we lived contentedly, without much trouble from the pine bark beetle. Eventually we moved to a bigger small town in Wyoming, one whose skyline encompasses the Snowy Range. When we were joined by an apple-cheeked child in a backpack, sharing the sight of an ice-crusted mountain lake and teaching him to leave a campsite clean became high priorities. He learned to cross-country ski amid sheltering pines, on skis that were barely longer than his father's forearm.

And now, all across the forest the trees are standing dead. Great swaths of red stain entire mountainsides, miles of forest roads, and views that were green last fall. Dead. And next year there will be more. The outbreak, we are told, is unprecedented. A million and a half acres on a map of Wyoming and Colorado is hardly less comprehensible to me than the present view from Kennaday Peak or the reflection in Silver Lake. Every tree in every direction is dead.

If I tell my son that the pine bark beetle is native to the Rocky Mountains and has long been a part of natural cycles, it does nothing to blunt the loss. Drought and warm winters have set the stage for this

Nothing about **this scale of ruin** feels natural. Our forest is a morgue.

attack, which is caused by the insects boring into the bark of their ponderosa and lodgepole hosts to lay eggs and complete their natural life cycle. Nothing about this scale of ruin feels natural. Our forest is a morgue.

The Forest Service publication *What's Eating the Trees?* says that during a beetle infestation more than fifty years ago, thousands of men walked the forest floor packing five-gallon tanks with hand-pumps, spraying every infested tree with a combination of fuel oil and insecticide, presumably DDT. "All that work didn't stop the beetle infestation," it says. "Cold weather in 1952 finally did." For us, that very cold weather may never return.

Chavawn Kelley *is a corporate communications manager for Western Research Institute. She lives in Laramie, Wyoming, with her bass-playing husband and fiddle-playing son.*

Lillian Heldreth

An Appalachian Idyll

I STAND ON AN ANCIENT MOUNTAIN IN THE AFTER-noon of the day and the year, when long, low rays of sun shine through the forest's leaves. The atmosphere itself seems full of light in every possible shade of gold and green. The quality of this light, passing through these trees I have known for over sixty years, defines my personal idea of the word "glory."

But coal, the original source of global warming, threatens to destroy my home and countless places like it more quickly than the actual rise in temperature will. Companies brag that "clean coal" can foster a greener environment plus energy independence. But the cheapest way to get coal is by removing mountaintops.

So each time I come here I sense the peril hanging over this place on a crest of Crooked Ridge in West Virginia. The surface of this land has belonged to my family for at least five generations and possibly more.

During my own seventy years, except for trees that might fall on the house, we've let this hundred acres grow up in native species—hickory, tulip poplar, maple, black gum, oak, beech, black walnut, and hemlock. I keep turning down offers to buy our timber, which is valuable ecologically and equally precious for its beauty.

To me, as to my father, each growing tree is a living sculpture, its form determined by the mountain's myriad microclimates and the infinite patterns of forest light. The hundred-year-old black oak in our front yard spreads an umbrella of arms; in deep forest, its sisters grow straight up.

The trees provide their own background music. We arrived the other night in the middle of a lively argument of katydids in quadraphonic cho-

To me, as to my father, **each growing tree** is a living sculpture...

rus. The next night a barred owl checked in with its "who cooks for you?" call.

"Gronk!" cry the ravens as they ride the morning thermals, and a pair of hawks cry "kee-yer," circling the ridge around midday. A pileated woodpecker has tried to fool me into thinking it's a flicker, but I have learned to distinguish its lower call. Sometimes the flicker drums on our metal roof—a wake-up call you can't ignore.

I want to pass these sights and sounds to my sons and grandchildren as a refuge for their spirits, as they have been for mine. But we don't own the mineral rights. Any day it chooses, a company can come and push our house, our trees, the very bones of the hills, down into the hollows, flattening Crooked Ridge, burying Brackens Creek, wasting the timber, which they don't even bother to harvest, and destroying at least ten homes on our ridge and in the valley below.

When I was a child, I thought this mountain was "forever." Now I am old. I do not know if the mountain and the trees will outlive me. I can only breathe to the sky my hope that I will stand here again in this glow of evening light.

Lillian Marks Heldreth *is a professor emeritus of English and Native American studies at Northern Michigan University. Born and raised in the mountains of West Virginia, which she still frequently visits, she lives in Marquette, Michigan, on the south shore of Lake Superior.*

Betty Owen

The Carson Range

Looking east from the mountains, you see a vast expanse of desert sagebrush and scrub, with a few clusters of piñon pine but none of the thick stands of conifers found at higher elevations. Some may see the desert as colorless and drab, but to me it is a **uniquely beautiful place.** I have lived here for almost twenty years and have watched the diminishing mountain snow pack, the long droughts, and the dropping water levels in the lakes.

Betty Owen, *who will celebrate her eighty-seventh birthday this year, lives in Carson City, Nevada. She is a widow, mother, grandparent, painter, and avid recorder of her nature walks.*

The Carson Range of the Sierra Nevada. Photo by Betty Owen.

Helen Whitaker

Bloomington Canyon

THE BEAUTIFUL MOUNTAIN AREAS OF THE BEAR LAKE Valley in southern Idaho have been my second home since early childhood. The old-growth pine forest of Bloomington Canyon, in particular, with its diverse plant and animal life, has been my nature lab. When I was growing up, the weather patterns and climate conditions remained fairly consistent from one season to the next. People could pretty much count on heavy snowfalls in winter, cold rains in spring and fall, and relatively mild temperatures in summer. Ever since the 1880s, when the area was settled by pioneers, there had not been a dramatic climate change that altered the lives of the canyon creatures and plants, and rarely did a weather event dramatically affect the area. All through the 1970s and early 1980s, when I was exploring the canyon on horseback, the weather patterns and climate conditions remained constant. One main landmark was an ancient Engelmann spruce tree, which scientists had estimated to be more than two thousand years old. I could always count on seeing that majestic beauty towering over the other trees as if surveying its domain.

In the mid to late '80s, however, the western United States moved into a drought cycle, and ten years into the drought, the weather in Bloomington Canyon changed drastically. There was very little snow during the winters, little to no rainfall in the spring and fall, and the dry, hot summers were 10 to 15 degrees warmer than I had ever known them to be. Water sources for plants and animals were drying up. Trees were dying and beavers were moving out of the canyon, but logging continued, just as it had since the days of

The canyon my daughter knows is very different from the canyon I knew at her age.

the pioneers. I didn't see how this forest could sustain itself under the drought conditions and continuous logging.

The severity of the situation manifested itself on June 3, 1998, when a microburst hit the area where the Engelmann spruce stood. Within a few minutes this tree and others, totaling 2 million board feet of lumber, had been felled. In the years since then, the climate of that area has remained much hotter and dryer than it was before the 1980s, and logging is still going on. The old-growth pine forest is giving way to the younger quaking aspens that took root where the pines used to be. How much more will the makeup of this canyon change as logging (which contributes to global warming) and the drought continue? The canyon my daughter knows is very different from the canyon I knew at her age. What will it be like when her children are growing up? I can only pray that nature will find a way to sustain itself in this beautiful place.

Helen Whitaker *was born and raised in Salt Lake City. She now lives in rural Lehi, Utah, and works as a paralegal.*

Dorothy Boorse

Prairie Pothole Wonder

ON A BRIGHT JUNE DAY I STAND AMID THE SHARP edges of the rice cutgrass, looking over a prairie pothole wetland. Circles of sedge, cattails, smartweed, and water plantain rim a puddle of muddy water. Green hues wash over me. I breathe the air, hear the call of the red-winged blackbird and the faint popping sounds of trapped air bubbles escaping from mud in the heat. Insects buzz, a goldfinch flicks by. A trickle of sweat on my temple evaporates in the breeze. The beauty of this day and this place stops me in my tracks. It is a holy moment, a moment of prayer. Nothing is more glorious than this wetland, this summer day, the joy of being allowed to do this research project for my Ph.D. I am transfixed.

Nothing is more **glorious than this wetland,** this summer day...

Today I am studying the life of these ephemeral pockets of water so critical to the health of the midwestern ecosystem. Some 3 million prairie potholes, scraped out by the grinding retreat of the glaciers during the last ice age, dot the upper Midwest in the United States and parts of Canada. More than 90 percent of them dry out regularly, and many have been degraded, plowed, dredged, or filled. Some potholes are protected, including thousands in the federal Conservation Reserve Program, a project funded to encourage farmers to keep wetlands out of agricultural use.

Today I am surveying the macroinvertebrates in a pothole on conservation land. As I sort my net samples, I know I will not find the unique fairy shrimp I would have seen a few weeks ago, because their short adult life span is over. I will, however, find dragonfly nymphs, small snails, and the tadpoles of various frogs, their development hurried in a race to leave before evaporating water strands them like raisins in a patch of baking mud.

Potholes, lying across the landscape like droplets flung by a giant, form a network of habitats that wink in and out, full one year, low the next. They support a disproportionate number of plant and animal species relative to their area. For example, 50 percent of North American waterfowl breed, feed, and nest in these small wetlands.

This habitat is vulnerable to climate change, which is likely to make this region drier, while economic pressure will cause some farmers to plow their drier seasonal wetlands. These twin pressures—increased use and decreased precipitation—are likely to further reduce these already limited wetlands.

My love of this place, which drives my teaching, writing, and personal decisions, translates into a passion to protect all such places. It is not only the big picture, the loss of the great flocks that once covered the skies of our continent, that burdens me. I want to prevent the loss of this one small space, this chapel, miniature and yet inestimably vast. Doing so is a work of love.

Dorothy Boorse *is an associate professor of biology at Gordon College, a small Christian liberal arts college in Wenham, Massachusetts. Her research focuses on wetland ecology.*

Richard Baker

One Acre at a Time

LIVING IN IOWA, WHICH HAS THE MOST ALTERED landscape of any state, I appreciate Aldo Leopold's statement about living in a world of wounds. All around us I see the effects of human use and neglect: endless monocultures of corn or soybeans, the loss of native plant communities to invasive species, intensive soil erosion and gullies, and stream pollution, which contributes to the Gulf of Mexico's dead zone. Global warming will only magnify these problems.

Eight years ago I had the good fortune to move out into the country, to 125 acres of woods, overgrown savannas, ponds, and fields. It was then that I saw a chance to make a difference.

It was then that I **saw a chance** to make a difference.

Leopold said that the first step in intelligent tinkering is to find all the pieces. Historical records helped me determine what the vegetation and landscape were like prior to European settlement. Our area had been a mosaic of prairie on the uplands, forest along the Cedar River, and oak savanna in between, with a scattering of springs and wet places. This mix had formed a very stable landscape with little runoff and erosion. My wife, Deb, and I decided that our best legacy would be to return the land to this pattern, restoring where we could and starting from scratch where that was necessary. This strategy will produce stable plant communities and landscapes even in the face of global warming.

In 2000 we planted a diverse mix of prairie species, such as compass plants and prairie blazingstar, on fourteen acres, the largest flat upland area on the property. In addition, we dammed the upper end of several steep valleys suffering from severe erosion. The dams allowed four small wetlands to form, which we planted with lovely local wetland plants, including wild iris, queen of the prairie, and arrowhead. Runoff and gully formation have virtually stopped, because the prairie sod retains so much moisture, and the wetlands act as holding ponds. Even the floods of 2008 had few adverse effects.

Aerial photographs dating back to the 1940s and 1950s showed some beautiful oak savannas, but these areas, left unmanaged for sixty years, became overgrown with tall trees. Eight years ago I began burning the understory and also cut many of the fifty- to sixty-year-old trees, leaving the open-grown savanna oaks. Some savanna understory plants are returning, and visitors are charmed by the beauty of this restoration.

It is a constant struggle to keep a handful of nonnative invasive species, like garlic mustard, autumn olive, and honeysuckle, from taking over the whole landscape. On the positive side, we are solving a number of problems, preserving our natural heritage, and preparing well for any future changes. The long walks I take every day convince me that I'm doing the right thing. Seeing the diversity and beauty of the prairies, savannas, and woodlands and of the birds, butterflies, dragonflies, frogs, and other wildlife gives us great joy. We have found most of the missing pieces of the mosaic, and paradise lost is becoming paradise regained.

Richard Baker *is a professor emeritus of geoscience at the University of Iowa. He and his wife, Deb, and two dogs live in the woods overlooking the Cedar River in eastern Iowa.*

Steel Creek

I don't know how big a difference we can make or how long it will take for the climate to respond to **our changes in behavior.** I do all the little things in the hope that decades from now I will be able to go to Steel Creek on a cold winter day, hear the **elks' hooves crunch in the snow,** and delight in romantic dreams of wilderness and great-grandchildren.

Amanda Keen-Zebert, *a native of northwest Arkansas, holds a Ph.D. in environmental geography. She lives with her husband, Konah, a nature photographer, in Fayetteville, Arkansas.*

Opposite page: Steel Creek, Buffalo National River, Arkansas. Photo by Konah Zebert.

John Calderazzo

The Lying Sky

THE SKY IS LYING TO ME AGAIN. I'M STANDING IN MY Colorado back yard, staring up at a dazzle of stars and imagining that the air I'm breathing stretches up and away from me for hundreds or even millions of miles, until the last lonely molecule of oxygen peters out in deep space.

Of course, this isn't true. I know that the atmosphere wraps our planet as thinly as a shell wraps an egg. But my eye is tricked by the transparency of air and the immensity of the universe, and my brain wants to follow. It's reassuring to think that air goes on and on, just as it's comforting to stand on a Pacific beach and assume that the crashing ocean is boundless, its amazing creatures numberless. Who wants to believe that the natural world can't absorb, unchanged, everything we throw at it?

... my eye is tricked by the **transparency of air** and the immensity of the universe.

But then I think about Yuri Gagarin, the Soviet cosmonaut who in 1961 became the first person to fly in space. As one story goes, Gagarin looked down shortly after liftoff, saw how thin the blue skin of the atmosphere really is, and became terrified. He had never before understood the limited and fragile nature of the only home we have.

Since then writers like Rachel Carson have shown us how pulling on just one thread in the complicated fabric of biological life can yank so many others out of kilter. But it seems we need to be reminded endlessly. How else to explain the tepid attention our policymakers and citizens have, until recently, paid to climate change? Ever-mounting evidence shouts that this may be the biggest single issue facing the planet.

So why haven't we acted? Scientific illiteracy? The fact that "Grow back the glaciers!" doesn't sound as sexy as "Save the whales!"? Eco-fatigue? Maybe the problem is that when I stare up at Orion or an afternoon thunderhead, I can't actually *see* anything getting warmer.

Or maybe our denial is born of an unfathomable clash of scales, as I've seen in people I've met over the years who live on the slopes of volcanoes. Refusing to leave even when the ground starts to rumble, they say, *It hasn't erupted in 1,200 years, so why should it start now?* Well, because volcanoes grow and collapse to the planetary beat of Deep Time, which reaches far beyond human generations. Thus, while my rational mind has long accepted the proofs of global warming, a tiny part of me *still* doesn't want to believe we puny humans are to blame.

Which is why we sometimes need to distrust gut feelings and pay attention to the bigger picture of science.

So here I am, standing in my back yard and watching an infinity of stars. And I'm thinking, *The thin skin of our planet is not immune to us.* The world is warming. We've caused it. And now, what are we going to do about it?

John Calderazzo *teaches creative writing at Colorado State University. With his wife, SueEllen Campbell, he founded and directs Changing Climates @ CSU, a lecture series in which professors talk about climate change from various academic perspectives.*

Tara Mitchell

The Price of Detachment

AS A LANDSCAPE ARCHITECT, I WORK TO CREATE landscapes of beauty and utility, shaping the land to satisfy the human eye and human needs. Yet very often I find myself restoring degraded landscapes, battling invasive plants, and seeking to preserve even the smallest of habitats—sometimes a single tree, which in its lifetime will hold thousands of birds, in whose universe millions of insects will eat and be eaten, among whose roots billions more insects, fungi, and bacteria make their home.

At a construction site, I see that the big oaks left unprotected near the work area are dead. Their naked limbs, like fingers, still reach toward the summer sun. The soil structure in the root zone has been crushed by trucks. People don't understand that soil is a living material, but it is alive only as long as it has biological connections. Once compacted, it can no longer hold air and water or sustain microorganisms. Without access to these essential elements in the soil, a tree will die. When it dies, not only does the immediate habitat disappear, but a link in the larger habitat is broken. The invisible is altered as well as the visible: nitrogen cycles, carbon cycles, microclimates, evapotranspiration—chemical and physical changes in water, soil, and atmosphere that, taken together, make the earth more or less habitable.

A few miles down the road, I pass a gap in the forest. Acres of soil lie bare. Bulldozers, backhoes, and excavators are eating away at the earth; a stream of trucks, like ants, cart soil away. It is like seeing flesh stripped, bone exposed. On the other side of the road, the landscape stretches low and flat, covered with stores, restaurants, and parking lots. Sparsely planted trees stir in the breeze above the hot concrete. Storm drains wait to pipe away rainwater. Very little is living here, yet we unquestioningly accept the replacing of forests with these lunar landscapes.

When we can no longer read the land, we no longer see what is in front of our eyes. Despite access to ever more information, despite threats of global warming, toxic water, and eroding soils, we continue to close our senses to the land. Our iPods shut out the rustling of leaves, the quiet of snow falling. Fences, measured strips of asphalt, rectangles of lawn, reshape the native landscape. Our taste for fast food kills the forest. Like global warming, our detachment will feed upon itself: as the climate warms, we will increasingly withdraw behind air-conditioned walls.

...we continue to **close our senses** to the land.

We have chosen not to live as an integrated part of the complex ecosystem upon which we depend, but to be separate, boxing ourselves off from cradle to grave. In so doing, we have lost the ability to sense both beauty and danger. We need to change, not for what we will lose in the future, but for what we miss in the moment. The landscape will always be here, whatever form it takes. Whether it is one we can live in may no longer be up to us.

Tara Mitchell *has been a landscape architect for the Massachusetts Highway Department for ten years. She lives in Medford, Massachusetts, and enjoys painting in watercolors, writing, and tending her orchids and bonsai.*

Bronwyn Mitchell

I Was Born on Shaky Ground

THE LAND THAT MAKES UP MOST OF LOUISIANA, AT least the southern part, consists of pieces of the Rocky Mountains, the Appalachians, and every place in between. Wind and water, snow and ice, work over time to break big rocks down into smaller and smaller rocks until the rock trades its former identity for that of soil. It can take five hundred years or more for an inch of topsoil to form.

Perhaps the mountain longs to see the sea, to taste salt water, to play witness to schools of fish, because as rock becomes smaller, it becomes more mobile. Driven by gravity, water falling onto the earth picks up whatever it can and moves it. In tributary after tributary, three quarters of North America drains into the Mississippi River through southern Louisiana.

When a river meets the sea, it slows down and spreads out into the traditional delta shape, which allows the sediment to fall out of suspension. In a geologic irony, the renegade sediment worn away from the mountains moves on to build up the land. This is southern Louisiana's unique story: five deltas and borrowed land. Beginning at the continental shelf, pieces of thirty-one states unite in a series of layers. When the sediments breach the water's surface, the coastal fringe is colonized by marsh grasses. The roots add structural stability, the live stems help capture additional sediment, and the decaying tissues continue the land-building process.

This is southern Louisiana's unique story: **five deltas** and borrowed land.

Rivers are dynamic. Always seeking the shortest route to the sea, they continually change course. People, on the other hand, like things to stay pretty much the same, so they build levees to control seasonal floods, thereby halting the periodic sustaining deposition of new sediment. When the Mississippi River tried to change course to flow west into the Atchafalaya River, the people responded by building the Old River Control Structure. This giant wall regulates water flow, sending a constant 30 percent to the Atchafalaya and 70 percent to the mouth of the Mississippi.

Louisiana is no longer growing. It is shrinking at a rate of one acre every fifteen minutes. Starved for sediment, the marsh is sinking into the sea. The rising sea level quickens the rate of sinking; even a few inches' rise is significant for a land below sea level.

Each summer, in a ritual as sacred as fireworks on the Fourth of July, my dad, along with all the other dads in the neighborhood, would order a load of soil. A big truck would dump what to a kid in New Orleans seemed like a mountain of dirt—five feet high—onto the front lawn. Armed with a wheelbarrow and shovel, we would use that mountain to fill in the areas around the house that had sunk over the previous year.

Southern Louisiana is the nation's canary in a coal mine. As Louisiana goes, so goes the country. Seventy-five percent of the nation's population lives in coastal zones. The question is, do we have enough shovels?

Bronwyn Mitchell *is a New Orleans native now residing in Baltimore, Maryland. A onetime women's professional football player, she is the executive director of the Maryland Association for Outdoor and Environmental Education.*

Racetrack Playa

When we learned that **nobody had actually seen the rocks in motion,** I recalled a quote by Henry David Thoreau, who said, "The finest workers in stone are not copper or steel tools, but the gentle touches of air and water working at their leisure with a liberal allowance of time." I returned to Death Valley in 2007 to present a public lecture on global climate change. I volunteer with The Climate Project, speaking to the public about the impacts of and solutions to climate change.

Mindy Kimball *is a major in the army, currently serving in Iraq as a space operations officer. A graduate of the U.S. Military Academy and California State University East Bay, she lives in Maryland with her husband and son.*

The "sliding rocks" of Racetrack Playa in Death Valley, California. Photo by Mindy Kimball.

Jennifer Kepka

Windmills, Talking

GOING BACK TO SEE MY FAMILY LAST SUMMER, WE drove past fields of fresh-cut Kansas wheat but also past fields of towering windmills, windmills so large they felt cartoonish—science fiction come to life on the broad prairie. There are dozens of them now, and hundreds more are scheduled to join them. They cut a scattered line from the smooth concrete interstate out to the edge of Lake Wilson, waiting to turn my state's most abundant resource—wind—into energy.

It's strange to see windmills here, in a county where every driveway has a pickup truck, where tractors still belch diesel fumes into hazy skies all summer, where field burning isn't up for debate, where recycling is the exception, not the rule. It's strange, and yet it's fitting, because it brings home the idea that global warming is really *global*, even for the places that aren't seeing the ocean rise or the smog thicken. The windmills rise out of land that the farmers of my father's youth didn't worry about conserving, land that is now managed mostly by men and women with agriculture degrees, those Future Farmers of America who have studied the best ways to fight erosion, pests, diseases. Now the windmills spin on their grazing pastures, and I think the farmers must see—must begin to understand—how interconnected we all are in the world. I wonder if they see these windmills, as I sometimes do, when they flip a light switch at night. I wonder if they hear, in the steady hum and whoosh of a windmill at work, the sounds of our cities being powered, our air being relieved.

My contributions to the fight against global warming are small. I reduce, I reuse, I recycle. But I also talk. Sitting in the cooling cab of one of those guzzling pickup trucks last summer, I found myself able, for the first time in my life, to connect with my farm-raised father on issues about the environment. We stopped in the shade of a grain elevator to marvel at the massive bulk of a load of windmill stalks sitting on a still train, and we talked honestly about the ways that energy use in our country has contributed to the carbon crisis. We talked about the need for these windmills, for more of these windmills, and he expressed real dismay that he wasn't able to put any on his farm because of recently passed state legislation.

The shadows of the windmills loom large in the prairie states. They are changing minds and attitudes simply by standing up, by working slowly and gently and steadily toward a goal. They are symbols that the farmers understand, and they are machines that give me hope. To talk about them is my best contribution; to encourage their spread is my greatest goal.

The shadows of the **windmills loom large** in the prairie states.

Jennifer Peters Kepka *was raised in the center of Kansas but now lives in Eugene, Oregon, where she is completing a master's degree in creative writing. Her hobbies include yelling at the TV news, forgetting to read the newspaper, and sending postcards.*

Tales from Urban America

Sarah Wolpow

At the Sign of the Heron, Turn Left

IF MY HUSBAND COOKED DINNER EVERY NIGHT, I would be delighted. Should Danish house elves visit in the wee hours and run the laundry, no problem. But offer me a car instead of my bike? Forget it.

I was twenty-three years old when necessity introduced me to my bicycle. No amount of time studying Boston's public transit maps yielded a solution that would take me between school and home and four different part-time jobs. Having access to a car wouldn't help, because parking was either nonexistent or so costly as to make working pointless. However, for a bookworm-and-glasses type like me, becoming a Boston bike commuter was a bit of a stretch.

On that first experimental day of my new biking life, I plotted a nervous course through the muggy morning to a path along the Charles River. And there, within minutes, I received a sign that I was on the right track—in more ways than one: a black-crowned night heron sat tucked into a clump of reeds facing the river. I'd never seen one before. As Boston's traffic sped by in its roller-coaster lanes, this exotic creature sat serenely in another world, looking for breakfast.

Later, heading home, I stopped to watch workers pulling up spent spring tulip bulbs. "Would you like a few?" they asked. A few turned out to be almost thirty, which they stuffed into every available pocket and which bloomed riotously in my garden for years. By the time I carried my bike down the basement stairs that night, I was hooked.

Oh, the sights you can **see from your bike** that you miss from a car!

Tens of thousands of miles later, I'm still enchanted. Oh, the sights you can see from your bike that you miss from a car! Oh, the good food you can eat after all that exercise! Oh, the ease with which you can park! Oh, the money you can save! Oh, the flocks of turkeys you can scatter as you coast down hills in the fall!

But putting aside the boundless passion of the converted, I recall myself to the theme of this book: the climate crisis. Transportation is responsible for more than a quarter of the greenhouse gas emissions in this country. To solve global warming, we must solve transportation. A Canadian task force on sustainability summed it up like this: our transportation system must meet people's needs, allow future generations to meet their needs, support a high quality of life, and be affordable, nonpolluting, technically possible, and powered by renewable energy.

The bicycle, the amazing bicycle, is all these things. A person on a bicycle is more efficient (in calories expended per pound and per mile) than any machine ever built and any creature that flies, walks, or swims. Can the bicycle meet people's needs? In the United States, less than one in a hundred trips is taken by bike, even though almost half of all trips are shorter than three miles. In the Netherlands, nearly one third of all trips are taken by bike. Go figure.

Sarah Wolpow *is a writer living in Brunswick, Maine, with her husband and two children. She worked previously as an environmental researcher and a statistics teacher.*

Reverse Migration

Dale Elizabeth Walker

IN THE NATION'S HEARTLAND, WATCHING THE SEASONS shift their timing and the wildlife alter their migration patterns, I began to question whether I had made enough of a commitment to environmental stewardship. Photographs comparing a week's supply of food for families around the world vividly demonstrate the massive size of the average American carbon footprint—not to mention our preference for suburban living, with stores, workplaces, and essential services just a drive away.

As a proponent of zero population growth, I brought only one child into this world. And with the example of a mother who crocheted plastic bread bags into functional doormats in the 1950s and '60s, I worked hard to recycle before it was trendy. My cellar would fill with bottles and jars until the semiannual trip to a local bottling plant yielded a few pennies per pound for the glass I would deliver. I also spent a few years sorting recyclables at a collection center, while most surrounding communities were slowly adding recycling to their trash service.

But with unimaginably vast sections of the polar icecap splintering off and melting into the ocean, I knew I had to do more. Even before the price of gasoline topped four dollars a gallon, I began to realize that my idyllic home at the rural edge of suburbia was a luxury the earth could no longer afford. Though I have spent many pleasurable hours in the park across the road, holding my breath as great blue herons soared over the ponds and deer fed in the meadows, I resolved to move within walking distance of my job so I would no longer face a forty-four-mile commute each day. The housing market is shaky, and I'm not sure I will be able to sell my beautiful home anytime soon, but within the week I am closing on a loft less than a mile from my office.

I have never been an urban dweller, although it is in my blood—my mother and father both spent their earliest years in large eastern cities. Now I look forward to a life on foot with a city to explore. A library, museums, entertainment venues, restaurants, shops, a farmers' market, and urban parks are just outside my new door. A large grocery will be opening six blocks away. Public transportation is also nearby.

It was the right time for me to reverse the historical American migration to wide-open spaces, to leave suburbia, with its miles of asphalt and traffic congestion, for the city lights. I will continue to recycle, although it will not be as convenient. My groceries will come home with me in cloth bags, and I will wear out a lot of shoe leather as I do one person's part to shrink what has become an unsustainable impact on the earth.

Now I look forward to **a life on foot** with a city to explore.

Dale Elizabeth Walker *is a mom and grandmother who has worked for nearly twenty-five years in the field of law, primarily as a law clerk. She lives in Kansas City, Missouri.*

Oracle

I see the health of our biosphere as the ultimate social-justice issue. **I paint and create** music to evoke feelings and affect behavior in ways that words cannot. When I show my work in art galleries, most viewers agree with the messages I try to convey, but some do not. I may not be able to change their minds, but I hope that the images I've created will stay with them.

Russell Brutsche *is an artist and songwriter living in Santa Cruz, California. His paintings have been featured in numerous shows in the United States and Japan.*

"Oracle," acrylic on canvas by Russell Brutsche.

Michael Gold

The Heat Is Always On

THE HEAT COMES UP THROUGH THE RADIATOR, filling my New York City apartment with warmth it doesn't need. It's mid-November and 60 degrees. The pipes are banging as the hot air, fired by oil, comes up from the boiler in the basement.

The building managers think that November is supposed to be cold (and who could blame them?), so the heat comes up as scheduled. I open all the windows to bleed off the heat and welcome the cool breeze blowing in.

The building managers think that November is supposed to be cold...

I hate the waste of it all. If the management could turn off the unneeded heat, we wouldn't have to burn so much oil, which will only make us all warmer in coming years.

The place where I work operates on an even more unnatural heating schedule, sometimes starting in October. The room I work in feels like a blast furnace, and I open as many windows as I can to cool off. Doesn't anyone realize that with our new warmer weather we don't have to turn on the heat so early?

My daughter, who is two years old, runs to me for a hug whenever she hears the pipes banging in our apartment.

"Scared," she says.
I ask her what's scaring her.
"Heat."
She thinks it's a monster. I think she's right.

Michael Gold *works and lives in Queens, New York. He and his wife, Frieda, have a two-year-old daughter, Miriam.*

Sarah Flanders

Apathy in the Inner City

In the urban world, climate change is difficult to grasp through direct experience.

AS A PSYCHIATRIST IN AN INNER-CITY CLINIC, I SEE firsthand why some people remain apathetic about the destruction of the natural world. Modern urban life for poor and working-class Americans means limited education, constant media messages to buy manufactured goods, and few connections to the natural world. Outdoor recreation and city park facilities have declined along with health care, work opportunities, and social safety nets for disadvantaged city dwellers. It is hardly surprising that so many feel no reason to join the fight against global warming.

In the urban world, climate change is difficult to grasp through direct experience. At one time Pittsburghers flocked to the city's parks on summer days and nights, drawn to a racetrack, boating pavilions, an outdoor ball park, and even car-camping spots. But these attractions are gone, and the green spaces of our city often stand empty. Manufacturing has largely left Pittsburgh, so the dusty, gritty industrial neighborhoods are cleaner now, but for many residents the concrete infrastructure is the only world they know. They spend much of their leisure time indoors, watching television or playing electronic games. With vastly less time outdoors, many people cannot see how their world is affected by climate change.

Grappling with poverty, not to mention trying to avoid dying from inadequate health care, is a full-time job for many of the patients I see. If you can't scrape together the bus fare to get to your doctor's office, how can you feel energized by the immense challenge of stopping the destruction of the natural environment? Many of my patients have little security in their lives; they see no reason to quit smoking, let alone try to curb global warming. Poor people in this country aren't ready to stop taking plastic bags from the store—why refuse what little you get that's free?

Pittsburgh is surrounded by miles of open land and forest, and people here imagine that the earth will continue forever just as it is; no one has yet built a memorial to everything that has already been lost. If the movement to stop global warming is to succeed, it will have to educate all Americans, not just those who live in beautiful places, about nature and the history of environmental damage. To draw people back outside into the natural world, we need to make fundamental changes, starting with improved health care and living conditions for those who live in our cities. Only then will it be possible to dispel their apathy and ask them to join the effort.

Sarah Flanders, *a psychiatrist, practices in Pittsburgh, Pennsylvania, where she lives with her family. She enjoys biking and gardening, and she volunteers as an urban ecosteward in Pittsburgh's parks.*

Gary Braasch

Above Portland

The tram, one of the latest elements in my hometown's **innovative transport system,** allows medical personnel, patients, and students to avoid an estimated 2 million vehicle miles a year in traveling to the medical school. The tram carries more than 100,000 passengers a month along 3,300 feet of cables at about 20 mph. It connects with a trolley and light rail system that extends to many suburbs and the airport.

Gary Braasch *is an award-winning conservation photographer living in Portland, Oregon. He is the author and photographer of* Earth Under Fire: How Global Warming Is Changing the World.

Above Portland. View from the top of the aerial tram at the Oregon Health and Science University. Photo by Gary Braasch.

Randall Curren

The Big Uneasy

A NATIVE OF NEW ORLEANS, I LIVED THERE UNTIL I was twenty-two, and I continued to visit until not long before Hurricane Katrina struck. In the first days after Katrina, I worried about displaced family members and friends unaccounted for. I remembered my mother carrying me home when a summer rain made the streets impassable, the water too deep for me to walk through. My neighborhood, Gentilly, was where the deepest flooding from Katrina occurred, but as a child I had no idea we lived in the lowest and most vulnerable part of town. When I was ten, I scavenged firewood for cooking in the days after Hurricane Betsy, which left us without power for many days.

When boats began rescuing Katrina victims in earnest after days of incomprehensible delays, I remembered riding out Hurricane Camille in a dormitory at the University of New Orleans, a few yards from Lake Pontchartrain and the London Avenue Canal, breached by Katrina. Camille had headed straight toward New Orleans and deflected to the east as it made landfall, sending a thirty-foot surge of water across Biloxi, Mississippi, much as Katrina did.

After Katrina, I began to feel that I would never be able to go home again. "Come and stay with us and I'll drive you around," my brother said a year after the storm. "But it's mile after mile of devastation, and I can't look at it myself without tears streaming down my face."

Once dubbed the "City That Care Forgot," the Big Easy is not so easy or carefree anymore. Before Katrina, no one on the Gulf Coast imagined they would ever see a hurricane as bad as Camille again. Water in the streets and narrow escapes during hurricanes

My brother's family **evacuated with little more** than a checkbook and a change of clothes...

were normal, and no predictions of Katrina's possible devastation could persuade New Orleanians that they would not be able to return home in a few days. My brother's family evacuated with little more than a checkbook and a change of clothes; it was eight months before they could reoccupy their home.

The human truth that Katrina made vivid for me is that our experience of what is normal leads us to discount objective evidence that something out of the ordinary is happening. The truth of climate disruption is that a major American city could be lost to the sea much sooner than people realize. In the thirty years between Camille and Katrina, the delta between New Orleans and the Gulf of Mexico lost 1,500 square miles of land mass, and the surface waters of the gulf warmed to a peak summer temperature of 90 degrees F. As oceans rise and warm, I fear that New Orleans will not be the only city more vulnerable to the bigger storms we can expect.

Randall Curren *is a professor of philosophy and department chair at the University of Rochester, where he holds a secondary professorship in education. Growing up in New Orleans, he divided his time between the library and the marshy woods near his home.*

Jennifer B. Freeman

Canceling Catalogs:
A Gift Whose Time Has Come

JUST BEFORE THANKSGIVING, MY FAMILY GAVE A holiday present to our New York apartment building. It started with a box in the lobby and a sign offering to cancel any catalogs that were put inside. Our plan was to encourage our neighbors to think a little and help save some trees.

To make a difference in the fight against global warming, you have to work on many levels: change your light bulbs, write to your senator, talk to your neighbor, and walk in the woods to remember what it's all for.

The next day the box began to fill up. Four inches of catalogs, then eight inches. Buried in the stacks we found Post-its bearing notes of gratitude.

At first the calling part was all me. My kids decorated the box, wrote the sign with colored markers, and carried the catalogs upstairs. But making phone calls seemed at first to be a grownup job. By the second week the volume was overwhelming. Catalogs come in an astonishing variety: children's clothing, smoked hams, toys, diamond jewelry, hiking gear.

On a day off from school, one of my sons dared to make a catalog-canceling call, to feel the prankish thrill of phoning a grownup and pretending to be someone else. Leo learned a lot that day: that it's better to talk to a live person, that you can ask for a live person even if the robo-prompt tries to steer you to an automated system, that you don't have to give your phone number just because a grownup asks you to.

That afternoon my older son joined in. The apartment sounded like a call center. "I'd like to be taken off the mailing list please?" "You mean the number in the yellow box?" "The first name is Caroline, C-a-r-o-l-i ..."

That day the members of our household canceled eighty-five catalogs on behalf of the neighbors. The project cost time and effort; each of us sacrificed. In short, it brought the true spirit of giving into our home. A slippery heap of canceled catalogs on the floor was tribute to our labors.

Every year, 19 billion catalogs are mailed in America. Catalogs use 3.6 million tons of paper, for which 53 million trees are cut down. Producing catalogs causes the release of 5.2 million tons of carbon dioxide into the atmosphere (equal to about 2 million cars on the road) and uses 53 billion gallons of water. People should be able to receive the catalogs they want, but they should cancel the ones they don't want. According to industry statistics, about 98 percent of catalogs go straight into the recycling bin or the landfill.

Doing **favors for the planet** is good for your soul.

Doing favors for the planet is good for your soul. Perhaps that's why our family continued to get notes like this one, from a friend for whom we canceled fifty-nine catalogs in a week. She said "I feel clean, purged, and righteous."

Jennifer B. Freeman *is a freelance science writer living in New York City. In her free time she enjoys taking nature vacations with her kids.*

Robert N. Shorin

I Love Muscle Cars, but I Hate My Own Hypocrisy More

YES! I LOVE THE SO-CALLED MUSCLE CARS, A CARRY- over from my youth in the 1950s, when hot rods and loud mufflers made me and my friends feel strong and cool and oh-so-grown-up. Of course I'm a grownup now, but I still like the sound of a hot V-8 engine revving up and gears smoothly hand-shifting from first into second, the aroma of exhaust, even the screech of rubber on the road as some fool peels off in a fast start to get to the next red light before anyone else. That may seem contradictory, I know, but that's who I am.

I'm one of the lucky ones who can afford to make some financial sacrifices and splurge on a brand-new Porsche Carrera. I test-drove one a few months ago with the serious intention of buying it. The acceleration was thrilling, as was the car's stability and the soft roar of the engine as I put this amazing vehicle through its paces on straightaways and around corners. Why stop there? I test-drove a hot new BMW, one of the Mercedes sports cars, and the fantastic Audi A5, which made my heart leap in ecstasy. *Vroom! Vroom!*

Just as I was about to buy or lease one of these fantastic pieces of vehicular engineering, my hypocrisy hit me in the eye. You see, I'm also an advocate of clean sources of energy, and I talk a lot about the environment to my friends. I take the high road and feel so good about myself and my moral position. I had just finished reading Lester Brown's *Plan B 3.0,* a well-researched scholarly book that documents the devastating effects of global warming on our planet, describing in scientific detail how climate change affects everyone, rich and poor alike, and what we can do about it. I've told my friends and relatives about the book and even bought copies of it for them to read.

So how the devil could I drive a high-powered gas-burning vehicle spewing exhaust fumes that will contribute to the earth's demise and ruin this planet before my grandson has a chance to enjoy it, just because I like the sound and feel of a hot car? No way! So I upped and got me to a Toyota dealer and leased the newest Prius hybrid. It drives very nicely, thank you. It gets me where I want to go, in style and comfort. It comes with every conceivable option. It is plenty fast, and its acceleration is more than adequate for any U.S. highway— I'm not racing at Le Mans. One of the benefits of the Prius is that I get around 45 mpg in the city and more than 50 mpg on the highway. Better yet, I backed my words with action, stopped being a hypocrite, made a small sacrifice, and did something to save our planet. I'm proud of me.

... how the devil could I drive
a high-powered gas-burning vehicle spewing exhaust fumes?

Robert N. Shorin *is a psychoanalyst and vice president of the Karen Horney Clinic in New York City. He lives on Long Island with his wife, Alene, who has been his best friend and supporter for forty-eight years.*

On Wildlife

Blake Matheson

Sea Bear

MASSIVE ANIMAL TRACKS—TWENTY INCHES FROM heel to claw—push deep into the blue ice, luminous and crystalline in the gold of the Arctic sun. They are the unmistakable marks of *Ursus maritimus*—the great sea bear.

A hard west wind rolls over my back, then ripples out over snow-choked lagoons and frigid reefs. The gray horizon is broken only by a towering crimson spike. When I move closer, I realize it is the nine-foot-long rib of a bowhead whale, slaughtered by Inupiats in September. Each year the ice retreats farther from shore, and soon the leviathans will be out of hunters' reach for the first time since man came to Barter Island.

The harsh and beautiful frontier we call the Arctic National Wildlife Refuge (ANWR) lies below me. In the summer months it is an expanse of warm russet tones rolling out from the roots of the mountains to the steely water of the Beaufort Sea. Beyond the Beaufort, few places carry men's names until the Arctic Ocean transits the earth's pole.

Now, in October, the auburn of the tundra has disappeared, succeeded by a white immensity broken only by black veins on the cracked heights of the Brooks Range and by the sun's ephemeral light.

I follow the bear's tracks toward the water's edge. Atop a whale vertebra the eyes of a snowy owl break the scene's gravity. Long-tailed ducks drift placidly in the last open water of fall. A flock takes flight, riding the wind to the southeast, the supple sound of air beneath their wings. I watch until they vanish in the opacity of a faraway mist.

From behind a rocky outcrop the old bear appears. Big shoulders propel his tremendous legs over swaths of gravel and ice, his stride unbending and stiff. Hunting has been difficult for him in recent years, and his blue-black lips hang loosely from a gaunt,

tired visage. Aged he may be, but the 1,200 pounds of carnivore before me is no less daunting for all his hard-won years.

The bear's head hangs low, then unexpectedly his eyes lift, meeting mine squarely, resolutely. A black fire burns deep within them, and he steps toward me. In the space between heartbeats, borne by ecstasy and silent terror, I know what it means to be human, to be vulnerable. He, too, knows what I feel. He has seen the terrified eyes of countless prey and savored the sweet, visceral smell of fear on the wind. But I am also aware of something else deep within, a stirring remembrance of man's ancient place below animals of exquisite and terrible power. After all, it was just such bestial jaws that chased man into witting evolution. To these creatures, as to our shared earth, we humans owe nothing short of *everything*.

A gull screams. The bear turns away, and gray cloud eclipses the Arctic sun.

The old male bear wanders through a maze of bowhead whale remains at Barter Island on Alaska's North Slope. Photo by Blake Matheson.

Blake Matheson *recently completed law school in Portland, Oregon. He plans to marry and to look for a job working on the legal protection of endangered species and their habitats.*

Curtis Childs

Tiny Scales

I ALMOST STEPPED ON IT, IT WAS SO SMALL. IT MIGHT have been a stick, lying on the sidewalk as the setting October sun shot red and gold through the oak leaves. But as I bent closer— look! Tiny scales! Could it be? The five-inch-long snake flailed and curled its soft body around my index finger as I picked it up. Every scale seemed flawless, thousands of miniature overlapping plates gliding across each other as the animal's spine articulated. Carefully lifting my hand, I turned my face to gaze at the orange-red under-side, confirming my guess.

A Michigan red-bellied snake. I hadn't held one since I was a child. My friends and I could catch two or three of them in a day, setting up bricks and rocks in the baby pool and putting the snakes in there just to watch and enjoy. Woods surrounded our subdivision then, and an hour's adventuring could lead the three or four of us to cornfields, swamps, and ancient stumps.

The red-bellies left when the bulldozers came. Even the big black garter snakes, which to my boyhood delight had haunted every corner of our yard, vanished. The wave of suburban development swept north from Detroit to crash over us, leaving in its wake strip malls and a gray satellite view when the froth finally receded.

The **wave of suburban development** swept north from Detroit to crash over us…

I peered more closely at the snake as insects hummed in the field. Somehow, the red-bellies had come back. These tiny, fragile reptiles had survived the overturned fields, the cement trucks, the pollution, and the drained wetlands—cosmic events to a creature this minute. But as I set her down, I looked up at the blue expanse of atmosphere overhead, suddenly aware of the magnitude of what the red-bellies might soon face. A pregnant female might move quickly enough to avoid a car's tires, but what would she do if statewide rain patterns shifted? Where will she hide if shorter winters trigger an ecosystem imbalance, and the invertebrate prey she needs to survive move away?

These little animals, so timid that they don't even try to bite when held, miraculously survived the turbulence of human development. Will that triumph mean nothing in a couple of decades? Can red-bellies, and thousands of other species like them, to whom a football field is a day's journey, do anything to grapple with the enormity of a changing atmosphere?

We can't know for sure, but as I watched the snake slip up over the curb into the grass, I smiled at the perseverance she stood for. Thanks for making it, thanks for the past you gave me, I thought, as scenes from years ago flashed across my mind. Now what future will I give you?

Curtis Childs *has a degree in communication from Oakland University in Michigan. He has been a disc jockey for his college radio station and a performing singer-songwriter.*

Lea Jane Parker

American Ruby-Spot Damselfly

I am an educator for a young people's environmental club in Arizona. As I lead a Nature Quest hike along the Verde River, I delight in seeing **young faces light up** when they find animal prints, damselflies and other insects, birds, plants, and interesting rocks. As they listen to the water's rushing music, they **learn about the impacts of global warming** and the need to protect ecosystems.

Lea Jane Parker *is a professor at Northern Arizona University, where she developed and teaches in the environmental communication program. She lives in Flagstaff, Arizona.*

An American ruby-spot damselfly alights on a reed above the Verde River in Arizona. Photo by Lea Jane Parker.

Daniel T. Blumstein

The Last Pika

I STUDY MARMOTS, BUT I WORRY ABOUT PIKA.
Although they look like small rodents, pika, known in Eurasia as
"mouse hares" and in the United States as "tundra bunnies," are
lagomorphs—relatives of rabbits, as close examination of their
teeth reveals. Pika live only on alpine and subalpine talus slopes. If
you're walking in a western alpine boulder field and worrying
about twisting your ankle, you may be in pika country. They make
a wonderful raspy squeal that sounds like a small squeeze toy. When
I'm trapping marmots on the talus slopes, I smile
when I hear those squeals, the pika's territorial signals and alarm calls.

I smile when I hear those squeals, the pika's **territorial signals** and alarm calls.

One part of my research focuses on how climatic
factors influence the behavior and survival of yellow-
bellied marmots in Colorado. I work with a population of marmots that has been studied continuously
since 1962. Some of my colleagues' recent work has
demonstrated that marmots are now emerging from
hibernation earlier in the year and that this change is
correlated with higher spring temperatures. Climate
change may thus influence the timing of the marmots' emergence.
I recently discovered that their social behavior also influences
emergence, a factor that may enhance or suppress the climatic effect.

Because I'm interested in how climate change may affect mar-
mot behavior, people ask me if marmots will be influenced by
global warming. My initial answer about the Colorado yellow-bel-
lied marmots is a guarded no. No, because these marmots live in a
10,000-foot range of elevations, from the foothills of the Rockies to
the top of almost every 14,000-foot peak I've climbed. (There they
collect a "summit tariff"—your lunch—from human invaders.)

No, because they live in a variety of habitats, and even with a drastic redistribution of habitats, which we anticipate global warming will generate, there will likely still be places for marmots to live.

By contrast, I tell people that I worry about pika. As the sagebrush climbs up the mountains and as tundra is lost to forest, I worry about where they will live and how they will find others of their species. Pika are habitat specialists, and it's the specialists that will be most negatively influenced by climate change.

Pika, Mount Rainier National Park. Photo by Brian Walsh.

I worry that my grandchildren will not have the chance to laugh with glee when they hear their first pika, that they will not be able to smile with fond memories of wonderful experiences in high alpine ecosystems, which are as threatened as their habitat-specialist inhabitants. I worry about the last pika.

Daniel T. Blumstein *is an associate professor and vice chair of the Department of Ecology and Evolutionary Biology at the University of California, Los Angeles. He lives in Los Angeles and Gothic, Colorado, with his wife and son.*

Susan J. Tweit

Where Are the Butterflies?

FOR THE PAST MONTH MY HUSBAND AND I HAVE hosted an accidental houseguest. She (or he—we can't tell at this stage) possesses an appetite so insatiable that we named her Gluttonous.

Her small size and single-minded quest for food allowed Gluttonous to remain unseen among the anise flowers I cut from our kitchen garden, even as she ate them. I spotted her munching on the bouquet several days later, balanced on multiple pairs of stubby legs—clearly a caterpillar, but one I didn't recognize, dressed as she was in wrinkled black skin speckled with white and red dots.

The next morning, the empty black gauze of that now-shed skin swung from a branch. Nearby the insect herself—surely plumper already—chewed steadily in her dazzling new skin; the green and black stripes studded with orange dots identified her as an eastern black swallowtail. Watching this unexpected guest pull an anise blossom to her mouth and eat, I remembered a friend's question: "Where are the butterflies this year?"

Our high-desert yard and kitchen garden usually attract five species of swallowtails, plus monarchs, sulfurs, painted ladies, fritillaries, western whites, and common blues. Anise swallowtails are normally so abundant that I plant extra anise in order to feed the plump caterpillars.

But not this year, when every butterfly has been cause for remark. Until this accidental houseguest, in fact, I hadn't found a

The accidental houseguest Gluttonous, an eastern black swallowtail caterpillar, munching a flower. Photo by Susan J. Tweit.

single swallowtail caterpillar in the garden. My plants had flourished unmunched.

What has changed? After a decade of increasing drought, this year's weather patterns oscillated wildly, bearing out the predictions for global climate change in our region. First came a winter snow pack so abundant that it broke records, and then nothing: no wet spring snow, no summer rain until it was too late to do any good.

...she would metamorphose just in time for winter, tricked by abnormal weather.

Watching our caterpillar houseguest chew another flower, I counted out the weeks and calculated that she would metamorphose just in time for winter, tricked by abnormal weather.

Over the next few weeks, Gluttonous ate her way steadily through the anise bouquet, growing larger and plumper by the day as autumn flared gold outside the windows. One morning she slung herself under a branch of anise, held by her stumpy pairs of hind legs and one glistening strand of white silk. Forty-eight hours later, her striped skin had hardened into a pale green chrysalis. The miracle of metamorphosis had begun—and snow painted the peaks white.

We debated what to do with our nascent adult eastern black swallowtail. She has no future inside or out. Yet she is the only butterfly our garden produced this year.

If this heartbreaking hatch of a single caterpillar, whose maturity comes too late to seed future generations, is the gift of global climate change, I grieve for us all. Because what we are losing is not just a single species but the thread of connection with the everyday wild that secures our place in nature's community.

Susan J. Tweit *is a plant ecologist by training and the author of twelve books, including her latest, a memoir titled* Walking Nature Home: A Life's Journey. *She lives with her husband in a house heated and cooled by the sun in Salida, Colorado.*

A Chambered Nautilus

Almost all mollusk shells are made of aragonite, a naturally occurring crystalline form of calcium carbonate. If we continue to follow the fossil-fuel-intensive scenario outlined by the **Intergovernmental Panel on Climate Change,** by 2060 the oceans will likely become so acidic that aragonite will start to dissolve.

Ursula Freer *is a painter and digital artist working in Sante Fe, New Mexico. Her work is primarily devoted to the beauty of the natural world.*

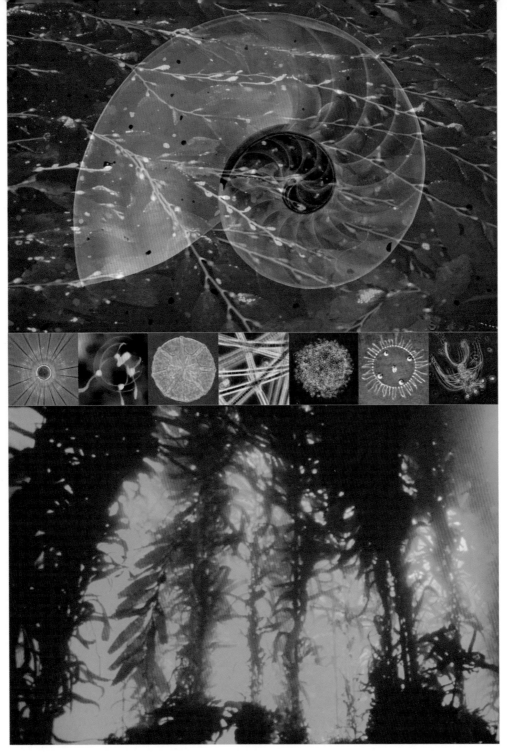

A chambered nautilus, Nautilus pompilius, *phylum Mollusca, class Cephalopoda. Digital collage by Ursula Freer.*

Sue Mauger

Salmon in Alaska

I HAVE WATCHED KING SALMON SWIM BY ME ON their return to the Anchor River; over Memorial Day weekend the Chinook wend their way past wader-clad fishers at the river mouth as they head upstream to spawn. They swim along a channel that continually reworks itself, shifting gravel bars, moving downed cottonwoods, searching for new angles of repose after the two hundred-year floods of 2002. The sediment-rich waters flow out of the Caribou Hills; snow is still melting from the two-hundred-square-mile watershed, which is virtually undeveloped compared to the Lower Forty-eight.

The returns of king salmon to the Anchor River have been strong, even though the forest has died. After the warm, dry summers of the 1990s, the bark beetles swarmed in dark clouds and ate their way across 1.4 million acres of the Kenai Peninsula. The dead gray trees that remain after the salvage logging and windstorms are a reminder of the forest that was.

I first stepped into the Anchor River in 2000, soon after the beetle infestation swept through. I came here in response to concerns from local citizens about the health of the watershed, to answer questions about whether the river could still support salmon after such dramatic change. I have now been studying this river for eight years, and what is most clear is that the change continues. My data tell me the river is warming.

Temperature data loggers show that water temperatures on the Anchor River, as well as on other salmon streams in south-central Alaska, are rising as air temperatures rise. Stream temperatures soared above 70 degrees F in the summers of 2004 and 2005. For families and communities that rely on salmon for commercial, sport, or subsistence fishing, this is ominous news, because high stream temperatures make fish increasingly vulnerable to pollution, predation, and disease.

The thought of warmer weather intrigues Alaskans. Who wouldn't welcome the prospect of summer walks on the beach without a parka? But the threat of warming winters clashes with the notion of healthy salmon populations. Climate change will eventually reduce our snow pack, shortening the snow-melt period that feeds our rivers. Then, with less water in the channels, summer stream temperatures will rise even faster. Our beloved salmon runs will suffer.

I moved to Alaska from Oregon, where salmon have succumbed to a long list of harms. Here on the Kenai Peninsula, we have a rare and important opportunity to make smarter decisions about land use and greenhouse gas emissions, decisions that will have a direct impact on the long-term sustainability of Alaska salmon. My work now is focused on providing communities and policymakers with the information they need to ensure that our magnificent stream systems, like the Anchor River, retain as much ecological resilience as possible in this time of unprecedented change.

> Here on the Kenai Peninsula, we have **a rare… opportunity** to make smarter decisions…

Sue Mauger *is the science director for Cook Inletkeeper, a community-based nonprofit organization focused on habitat and water-quality protection. She lives in Homer, Alaska.*

Dolphins in the Water off California

Dolphins are vulnerable to global warming even if the effects on them are not immediately evident. **Changes in weather patterns** and the ocean's increasing acidification as it absorbs more and more CO_2 is likely to disrupt the habitats and distribution of the dolphins and their prey. Even increasing susceptibility to disease—as my own studies reveal—lowers reproductive success, and survival rates are linked to a warming ocean environment.

Maddalena Bearzi *is president of the Ocean Conservation Society and coauthor of* Beautiful Minds: The Parallel Lives of Great Apes and Dolphins. *She lives in Marina del Rey, California.*

Dolphins in the water off California. Photo by Maddalena Bearzi.

David Beebe

A Beautiful Shrimp

I CAN'T HELP IT. THE CLOSER I LOOK, THE MORE I'M drawn in. This spot shrimp came from hundreds of feet below the dark waters of southeastern Alaska's Alexander Archipelago—a place where the sun, as well as our awareness, truly does not shine.

At first glance, the spot shrimp comes off as almost cartoonish—or otherworldly. Then, after taking in this creature for a few seconds, I'm taken aback by the exquisite intricacy of its luminescent compound eyes, its striped and segmented legs and beautifully marked shell, all composed of the seemingly impossible melding of carbon and calcium molecules suspended in the sea, which somehow coalesce into an exquisite structural form of utility, complexity, and beauty.

> At first glance, the spot shrimp comes off as **almost cartoonish—** or otherworldly.

Yet because of global warming, in the acidified oceans that scientists say are only fifty years into our future, this kind of shell will dissolve before it fully forms. Our oceans have always played the important role of absorbing carbon dioxide from the air. But because of the rapid increase of carbon dioxide in our atmosphere through the use of coal and petroleum products, deforestation, and forest fires, our oceans are becoming more acidic.

I can't help it. The more I hear about ocean acidification, the more concerned I become. It is time for a much greater awareness of this debacle. Most humans' appreciation of marine ecosystems stops at the reflections from the surface of the water and resumes at their dinner plates. My job as a commercial fisherman starts where most people's vision stops, just below the surface of the water, where I pursue and capture the largest of intact ecosystems for the world's dining tables. As a fisherman, I'm fated to be among the first to witness what happens in our oceans in the coming years, perhaps one of the first to glimpse firsthand the full magnitude of impacts on the planet from acidified oceans.

According to recent studies, ocean acidification from unchecked global warming threatens marine ecosystems that supply food for over half of the world's population. If scientific calculations are correct, and we have every reason to believe they are, ocean acidification will create catastrophic changes, leading to a famine of unimaginable proportions. Fortunately, we can avoid this catastrophe if we act quickly to reduce carbon emissions. Here's hoping a greater public awareness of global warming and ocean acidification will keep our marine ecosystems intact so we can continue to feed the world.

Spotted shrimp, Alexander Archipelago, southeastern Alaska. Photo by David Beebe.

David Beebe *is a Vietnam-era veteran who has worked as a commercial fisherman for the last twenty-five years. He lives in Petersburg, Alaska, in the heart of the Tongass National Forest.*

Faith and Conventions

VI

The Golden Rule

Matthew, Nancy, and Emma Sleeth

I USED TO BE A PHYSICIAN—THE CHIEF OF STAFF AND head of the emergency department—at one of the nicest hospitals in America. But I felt as if I were straightening the deck chairs on the *Titanic*, saving one patient at a time while the whole ship—the earth—was going down. Today I am one of a growing number of evangelical Christians whom the Lord is using to witness to people about his love for them and for the natural world.

The Golden Rule allows us to see the moral side of many issues, including environmental ones like global warming. Love thy neighbor as thyself: one cannot ignore the Golden Rule and claim to be a Christian. It isn't a suggestion or a guideline; it is a commandment from God. What is the connection between the Golden Rule and the environment? Aren't our choices of homes, cars, and appliances just a matter of lifestyle, not a moral or spiritual matter? Does God care whether I drive an SUV, leave the TV on all night, or fly around the world to go skiing? The Bible doesn't mention any of these things; they didn't exist in Jesus's time. Yet Jesus taught us to follow the spirit of the law, not the letter. From the spirit of the law and the example of his love, we can determine the morality of our actions.

—Matthew Sleeth

When Matthew suggested that he wanted to give up his successful medical career to "save the planet," my stomach turned inside out thinking about what we might lose—our beautiful home, our harborside neighborhood, our vacations, not to mention health benefits and a retirement plan.

The selfish part of me began to whine: what about the many years of undergraduate school, medical school, and residency we had gone through together? Wouldn't he be wasting all that training? And there were the practical concerns: our kids were approaching their teen years, with college just around the corner. How could we possibly save enough money to pay for their education if our income dropped to zero? How would we put food on the table?

But we took Jesus's advice and began cleaning up our own act before trying to clean up the rest of the world. Over the next couple of years, we gave away half of our possessions and moved to a house the size of our old garage. Contrary to our fears, we found that the more we "gave up" in material things, the more we gained in family unity, purpose, and joy. Eventually, through many small changes, we reduced our electricity use and trash production by nine tenths and our fossil-fuel consumption by two thirds. **—Nancy Sleeth**

I remember when my best friend Hannah cut off a foot of her hair. I thought I'd never get used to it. For the next month, every time I saw her I was once again surprised to see gentle waves of brown curling about her ears, too short to pull into her customary ponytail. But after a while Hannah's short hair began to seem normal. Now I have a hard time picturing Hannah *with* long hair.

The same forgetting can happen with global warming. The first time we read about the effects of climate change, we immediately commit to carpooling more. But soon we lose our enthusiasm, and pollution again seems normal, greenhouse gases unavoidable. Loss of zeal really means loss of heart. To make a difference, we have to care about the people affected by the environmental changes—and about the God who calls us to do something about it. **—Emma Sleeth**

> ...we took Jesus's advice and **began cleaning up** our own act...

Matthew Sleeth *is the author of* Serve God, Save the Planet: A Christian Call to Action *and the introduction to* The Green Bible. **Nancy Sleeth**, *a former communications director for a Fortune 500 company, is the author of* Go Green, Save Green: A Simple Guide to Saving Money, Time, and God's Green Earth. **Emma Sleeth** *is a junior at Asbury College and a leader of the evangelical movement to prevent climate change. She wrote* It's Easy Being Green *when she was fifteen. The Sleeths live in Wilmore, Kentucky.*

Nez Residence, Tó'sido, New Mexico

This is our **ancestral land.** To the south, Bennett Peak and Fort Butte jut out of the desert, and to the north, Tsé Bit'a'í (Rock with Wings) reaches into the sky. The Four Corners power plant and the San Juan generating station rank high in releases of nitrogen oxide, carbon dioxide, and mercury. Yet the Environmental Protection Agency has authorized dynamiting and drilling here for the Desert Rock coal-fired plant. A small group of warriors has protested, but the Navajo Nation's president says the plant will be good for his people. It is not good for the animals, plants, rivers, sacred mountains, and future generations.

Vangee Nez, *Diné, from Tó'sido, New Mexico, is of the Red Streak Running into Water Clan. She is pursuing a Ph.D. in language literacy for indigenous language revitalization.*

Nez residence, Tó'sido, New Mexico. Photo by Vangee Nez.

Laura Pritchett

Dumpster Diving:

My Day of Saving 66 Million BTUs

ONE OF THE REASONS I FIND MYSELF IN A DUMPSTER in my Colorado town has to do with the changing climate. Usually my two children are in the dumpster with me, and usually we're looking for aluminum, the most abundant metal in the earth's crust. The symbol for aluminum is Al, and its atomic number is 13, but its most important characteristic is this: it is too chemically reactive to occur in nature as a free metal, so it gets locked in with other elements, mainly in the form of bauxite ore, and freeing it takes an incredible amount of energy.

Basically, when you hold an aluminum can in your hand, you're holding a bit of a strip mine and its accompanying piles of tailings, a power plant, and a smelter; you're holding bits of boats and trains and the fuel required for transportation; you're holding can- and soda-making factories.

> ...when you hold **an aluminum can** in your hand, you're holding a bit of a strip mine...

While digging out beer cans from the dumpster, I consider the facts. Recycling the aluminum in cans takes 95 percent less energy than freeing it from bauxite. One pound of aluminum makes about thirty cans, and each can requires about 3,000 BTUs. So for every two or three cans we recycle, we basically save one pound of coal. It sounds complicated, but it's not. Not when you consider what three cans means in the bigger picture of a clean, pure sky.

After digging in the dumpster for hours, my young son declares that it's "metal-run time." In fact, we are overdue at the recycling center, and there's so much metal in the bed of my old pickup that it looks like a crazy robot, arms and legs sticking out monstrously, threatening to attack the normal cars that dare come near.

While the guys at the center unload and weigh the metal, I entertain the kids with sidewalk chalk: we sit down on the blacktop to draw pictures of the earth and sun and shooting stars. We draw an entire universe, bright and healthy-looking.

Finally, the workers are done: we have 108 pounds of cans, 400 pounds of scrap aluminum, 10 pounds of copper, 174 pounds of radiators, 116 pounds of insulated wire, 25 pounds of soft lead, 23 pounds of stainless steel, 30 pounds of yellow brass, and a bunch of batteries.

If a coal-fired power system were used to produce that amount of aluminum, it would release 18,000 pounds (9 tons) of carbon dioxide into the air. That's 56 million BTUs, which we've saved by recycling. Then there's the copper—from the wire and radiators—which saves another 10 million BTUs and keeps an additional 3,000 pounds of CO_2 from being emitted. And we're talking just about the aluminum and copper here; we're not even including how much earth would have been stripped, processed, and laid waste.

Before we leave, I suggest to the kids that we go dumpster diving again. They let out a cheer, and so does a mountainside and the sky. At least I like to think so; it's enough to keep the heart happy.

Laura Pritchett *is the author of a novel,* Sky Bridge, *and a collection of short stories,* Hell's Bottom, Colorado, *which won the PEN USA Award and the Milkweed National Fiction Prize. She lives in Bellvue, Colorado.*

Donald Hoyle

The Energy of Creation

NOW A RETIRED CLERGYMAN, I STILL REMEMBER, from my seminary days in the early 1960s, a Franciscan monk who addressed the class. He said that the most important thing is to get your doctrine of creation right, and that if you do, all else will fall into place. I believe he was right, so I hope we will go back to using the natural, God-given sustainable energy from the sun, wind, water, and heat from the ground. Then we will be in accord with the doctrine of creation.

We live in a time when the distribution and uses of energy are way out of balance and supply. As Mahatma Gandhi said, "The good Creator has put enough resources in creation to take care of man's need but not enough to satisfy man's greed." Germany's secretary of energy once pointed out, when asked how the developing countries would meet their needs in this time of energy shortages and crises, that we all have sun, wind, water, and geothermal energy available, no matter where we live on this planet. Although some places have insufficient water, abundant supplies of the other renewable energy sources can be harnessed.

My own adventure in this time of energy shortages started when I replaced my oil-fueled baseboard hot-water system with geothermal energy from an existing artesian well. I have what is known as a "dump" system, in which water from my artesian well circulates through the system and returns to the ground by way of an existing hand-dug well.

What we need to do is **start thinking** outside the box...

After putting in the geothermal system, I realized that heating and air-conditioning my house would require a lot more electricity. Luckily, I am blessed with a south-facing home that provides considerable passive solar heat and light. By installing photovoltaic panels on my roof, I was able to fulfill all my electrical needs, and I am now self-sustaining.

I believe God has provided for the energy needs of creation. What we need to do is start thinking outside the box by working in accord with the natural cycles of nature rather than seeking to rape the earth to satisfy our insatiable greed.

Donald B. Hoyle *is a retired United Methodist clergyman. He lives in Mansfield Center, Connecticut, with his wife of forty-eight years.*

Howard V. Hendrix

The Other Part of the Equation

MY WIFE AND I HAVE HAD A TASTE OF A BETTER future. We've been lucky enough, worked hard enough, and made enough sacrifices that we are now able to live where we choose: in the Sierra Nevada, just shy of 5,000 feet in elevation.

We can see the Milky Way at night and breathe without coughing up lung slugs, but it's no simple Shangri-la. Living here is not easy, which may be why more people don't choose the far exurban life.

And even here we are not immune to the effects of global warming. Neighbors who have long lived here tell us about new phenomena they've never seen before—not just unusual weather but also unexpected flora and fauna. Poison oak, long prevalent in the foothills but extremely rare in our higher forests, has become more common up here. Another foothill species, the tarantula, recently showed up in a neighbor's driveway. We hope it hitched a ride on a truck from the valley, but we suspect the big, slow-moving spider is a harbinger of the "species creep" that's coming to our neighborhood.

We are part of that species creep, too. Not just those of us who dwell in old, cut-over timberland, but all humanity. Living in a California forest throws into high relief one aspect of this situation: our species' million-year dalliance with fire. Together, humans and fire have burned their way clear around the globe. Applying the ancient technology of fire to the ancient sunlight of fossil fuels is but the latest intensification of our relationship. As surely as playing with fire is like having unprotected sex, global warming is the unintended conse-

> Together, **humans and fire** have burned their way clear around the globe.

quence—the unplanned pregnancy—of our long love affair with ourselves, our technologies, and our dominion over the earth.

My wife and I do what we can. We own a hybrid car and try not to drive "off the hill" more than three days a week. Our house is built in such a way that we don't need air conditioning. Nearly all our household heat comes from burning, in a superefficient wood stove, the short-term carbon derived from our overcrowded second- and third-growth trees. We're also returning our forest to pre-1850 conditions by burning selectively and by chipping understory thickets and letting the chips decay in place.

The most important thing we've done to shrink our carbon footprint is deciding not to have children, a choice that may have value not only for our household but also for the larger household of the earth. Worldwide, although smaller families currently tend to consume more energy-intensive resources as their wealth increases, it's also true that the shelter, food, and water required by each additional person enlarges a family's carbon footprint—regardless of the family's wealth or poverty.

I'd feel better about the future of life on earth if both the size of our overall human family and our use of resources were not ratcheting up as fast as they are. Until we address both parts of the equation—not only hyperconsumption (by living more simply and using nonfossil energy) but also hyperpopulation (by voluntarily reducing birthrates)—all our "greening" will amount only to spraying slightly less flammable green paint on a forest fire.

The life my wife and I have chosen is not for everyone, but, together with other families choosing other variants, we may be able to keep from "burning down the house."

Howard Hendrix *has taught literature at the college level for many years and has written science fiction, political essays, and literary criticism. He and his wife live in Pine Ridge, California.*

Lewis Ziska

Monetary Capital, Biological Treasure

RECENTLY I HAD LUNCH WITH A SCIENTIST COLLEAGUE who had been active in presenting data on the perils of global climate change to world leaders. He told me that without fail, at the end of a presentation, policymakers would approach him separately and ask quietly, "But my country won't be affected, right?"

I asked how he responded.

He smiled. "The ones who ask the question are from North America and Europe," he said. "The ones who consider themselves rich—who think they won't be impacted by global change."

"Do they have a point?" I asked.

He sighed. "Rich is relative. There is monetary capital, and there is biological treasure. You understand the difference?"

I thought about this. Money after all, did put food on my table. But then again, so did biology. I stared at my fork. A piece of tomato was stuck to a lettuce leaf.

"Tomatoes," I said, "are native to Peru, the lettuce originally from Iran." I took another look at my salad. "The cucumbers came from Armenia, the radish from China."

I have been a scientist with the U.S. Department of Agriculture for almost twenty years. I know that if you could look beyond the shelves of the supermarket to see the evolution of food, you would be amazed.

...look beyond the shelves of the supermarket to see **the evolution of food,** you would be amazed.

I know too that 75 percent of the world's calories comes from only a dozen crops: barley, maize, millet, oats, rice, sorghum, sugar cane, wheat, white potatoes, sweet potatoes, cassava, and soybeans. None of these crops (except for an ancestor of corn) are indigenous to North America or Europe, the "rich" continents.

If humankind is to find itself in the face of global climate change, we must find varieties of these crops in their native lands that can adapt to extreme temperatures, drought, new weeds, pests, and diseases. Only in biological diversity, the treasure of the "poor" countries, are we likely to find ways to feed the one billion additional people expected to be born in the next decade.

Yet this very treasure is at risk from climate change. The wealth of developing countries lies not in their commercial banks but in their land—land that supports most of the globe's biological diversity, treasure that will be sold to offset the economic cost of coping with climate change. And it isn't just food. Flowers, herbs, fungi, medicines—all are at risk.

Did I understand the difference between money and wealth?

"I get it," I said, putting down my fork. "But what do you actually say to them?"

"I tell them that if they just fend for themselves, all of us will be the poorer for it."

Lewis Ziska *is a plant physiologist with the USDA's Agricultural Research Service in Beltsville, Maryland. He is investigating the role of increasing carbon dioxide and changing climate on food security, invasive species, and aerobiology.*

Peddling Solutions to Climate Change

My colleague Bill and I **pedaled five thousand miles** across the country, peddling solutions to climate change. We made fifty presentations at schools, businesses, and community centers and gave dozens of radio, TV, and newspaper interviews. One student we talked to led a fight against a coal-fired power plant in her community. Others found ways to become more energy efficient, such as by changing their light bulbs or bicycling to work.

David Kroodsma, *an expert on the carbon cycle, has worked at the Carnegie Institution for Science. The founder of Ride for Climate, a bicycle-based climate education project, he lives in Oakland, California.*

David Kroodsma at a wind farm in South Dakota. Photo by Bill Bradlee.

Counting Cranes

John F. Wasik

EVERY APRIL I COUNT CRANES—SANDHILL CRANES, to be precise, which have red heads, elegant necks, and majestic wingspans. They were once endangered because their wetland habitats were drained and they were hunted for their plumes. They are my personal indicator species for the health of the environment. As the birds return to their local wetlands in ever-greater numbers in the spring, I try to transform my *personal* habitat into a more environmentally friendly place.

My family of four and I have always been conscious about environmentally sound living. Since I work mostly at home and live in a conservation-minded community, my local-transportation carbon footprint is almost nil. Yet there's so much more we need to do as we become increasingly alarmed about melting icecaps and polar bears struggling to survive.

Making pledges and listing action items keeps us on the path of climate-change awareness, but as an amateur naturalist, I wanted to measure how our family was doing. When I ran our basic lifestyle through the EarthLab carbon calculator, I found that while we were pouring somewhat less carbon dioxide into the atmosphere than the average Illinois or U.S. resident, we were still producing 13.4 tons annually! I didn't feel good about that, and I suspect the lion's share was generated by the tens of thousands of miles I spent in an airplane last year.

The little steps we were taking were certainly helpful but not dramatic in the bigger scheme of carbon-dioxide release: turning off lights, eating locally, taking shorter showers, using cloth napkins (and washing them for reuse), composting kitchen waste, using leftover plastic shopping bags for garbage (and bringing our own bags to the grocery store), buying biodegradable cleaning products, washing clothes in cold or warm water, and taking public transportation.

I'm pledging to grow more food in my back yard and buy more locally grown meat and produce. I can use my own compost and mulch on the gardens and freeze what we don't eat, as I usually do with our tomato crop. I'm adding to our winter stores by growing potatoes, Swiss chard, and Brussels sprouts. I'm going to monitor our energy use and try to do low-tech things like hanging clothes outside to dry and getting old-fashioned window shades for the south windows in our family room. We are replacing the 65-watt can lights in the basement with 16-watt dimmable compact fluorescent bulbs. Nothing my family does, though, will amount to much unless all vehicles, homes, factories, and offices are built or rehabbed to be energy efficient. So I will urge my elected representatives to extend and increase tax credits for energy-efficient and energy-producing buildings and transportation. We must have mandatory national energy standards.

Lobbying may be the most effective way to help the earth. It's virtually carbon neutral and will get our industrious nation to come up with a comprehensive plan. Before you can fly, you need to flap your wings a lot.

> Lobbying may be the **most effective way** to help the earth.

John F. Wasik *is an author, journalist, speaker, teacher, and activist. His neighborhood in Prairie Crossing, Illinois, has open space, an organic farm, restored wetlands, prairies, and trails.*

View from the Yakama Nation

Moses D. Squeochs, as told to Rebecca Hawk

I AM A FULL-BLOODED YAKAMA INDIAN, AND I PRACTICE
the traditional ways of our people: fishing, hunting, and gathering
roots and berries. The Almighty placed our people in the Pacific
Northwest region of this continent, along with everything else that
is here to sustain us—the flora, fauna, aquatic life, waterways, and
land. Our rights to inhabit our reservation lands and ceded terri-
tory—a mere remnant of our original homelands—and utilize the
resources within it are based in a fundamental, solemn treaty
agreement with the United States.

Since time immemorial we have survived on this continent,
but in the last four hundred years we have suffered greatly from
the influx of immigrants who have a different relationship to the
earth. They brought our people to our knees through wars, disease,
and dislocation, and in my own generation, they sent us, as young
men, away to boarding schools. The goal was to "kill the Indian
but save the man." As they attempted to kill the *Indianness* in us
and make us more like them, they taught us the Manifest Destiny
doctrine: a God-given right to do what one wants with the land for
one's own benefit, with little or no regard to the sustainability of
anything or anybody, even oneself. For a time, some
of us contributed to the living out of this doctrine
and the careless misuse of resources. But our elders
taught us to honor the land and water, so we were
not completely converted to the way of thinking
that was imposed upon us.

…our elders taught us to **honor the land** and water…

Today most of our people live in stick houses.
We drive vehicles and use cell phones. We live
within and enjoy the benefits of a modern society, but we also suffer from new threats to our health and well-being. Our people are
dying of cancers and other diseases at rates higher than those of

the general population because we still live close to the land and water, which are now polluted.

The rapidly warming climate is putting stress on our fish, animals, plants, and berries, and these resources are all diminishing. As we lose our healthy food supply, we have nowhere to go to sustain ourselves. But we now see in our young people a determination to honor our traditional cultural and spiritual ways of life and to stay connected to the land. As elders, we are trying to carry ourselves in such a manner that the young people of the next generation will live with respect for this place.

Moses Dick Squeochs *is the general council chairman of the Confederated Tribes and Bands of the Yakama Nation.*

Rebecca Hawk *is the regional air-quality coordinator for the Yakama Nation.*

Ray Trimble

Stewards of the Earth

MY MOTHER WAS A DEEPLY RELIGIOUS WOMAN with an intense social consciousness. She spent her life helping people less fortunate than herself, while also maintaining an abiding concern for those yet to be born. She often emphasized the biblical injunction that we must be stewards of our God-given earth.

When she died, my mother left a modest inheritance that my wife and I decided to invest in the future of our planet. We replaced our two cars with hybrids and purchased forty-five solar electric panels for the roof of our home.

> The point is that we have **significantly reduced** our carbon footprint.

It is with some embarrassment that I confess we use far more electricity than we should. We are a large extended family living under one roof, and we use our electric dryer heavily. We have an electric range in the kitchen and an air conditioner that runs for long hours during our hot summers. Before installing the panels in late 2006, we were purchasing about 50 kilowatt hours (kWh) a day, averaged over the year, from our utility. Our total usage increased slightly in 2007, but more than 60 percent of that was free, from our own roof. Our utility had to generate less than 23 kWh/day for us. In 2008 we did even better, buying an average of less than 16 kWh/day.

I have no idea how long it will take for the investment to pay off on an accrued-interest basis or whatever it is the accountants like to talk about. That is not the point as far as I am concerned.

The point is that we have significantly reduced our carbon foot-print. To put it in my mother's terminology, we are now better stewards of the earth, doing at least a small part to provide a more livable planet for generations to come.

Ray Trimble *spent most of his career as a computer programmer at IBM. Now retired, he lives in Morgan Hill, California, with his family.*

For Tomorrow

A Teachable Moment

Frank Schwing

> Human history becomes more and more a race
> between education and catastrophe.
>
> —*H. G. Wells*

AS AN OCEANOGRAPHER AND CLIMATE SCIENTIST, I have had the opportunity to witness and play a part in the research that has built an overwhelming case for human-caused climate change. The science community has the responsibility to inform the public about the rapid changes occurring in our climate, to foster a scientifically literate electorate, and to educate tomorrow's citizens and leaders about the perils of not acting swiftly and comprehensively to reverse the forces driving global warming.

I have given dozens of public presentations and lectures, many of which our son and daughter attended. Even in grade school they could explain the mechanisms of global warming. At a beach party they were able to study the waves and warn us all that the rising tide would sweep away our fire (yes, it really happened!). My wife and I have taken advantage of numerous "teachable moments" to talk about climate change, such that it has become a running family joke; "Science Talk with Frank Schwing," our kids would proclaim whenever I began telling some story about science in the everyday world.

As I approach the later stages of my scientific career, I could define my legacy in a number of ways. I've been fortunate to serve as a researcher and manager in a federal agency dedicated to understanding climate change and guiding our nation's efforts to address its effects. With a cadre of talented colleagues, I've published scientific papers, helped plan our national climate-change research program, and reviewed international climate assessments. My family has two hybrid cars, and this year we installed a solar-power generating system for our house.

But my greatest legacy is a living one. Eye-rolling and joking aside, our children, now young adults, recognize—as do many others I've encountered—that the consequences of climate change will be their unfortunate inheritance. They also understand that dealing with and solving this global problem will be theirs. My wife and I share a great pride, not only in what they have learned, but in the joy with which they pursue scientific truth and their appreciation of the urgency of creating a scientifically literate public.

...my greatest legacy is a living one.

Our children will carry on the fight to slow and ultimately reverse global climate change because no one else can do so; there is no other option. I look at their young, confident faces, and I, too, am confident that they will succeed.

Frank Schwing *is an oceanographer with the U.S. National Oceanic and Atmospheric Administration and director of the Environmental Research Division of the NOAA Fisheries Service. A native of West Virginia, Frank resides in Monterey, California.*

The Burns Homestead

Our home is a piece of art and **a work in progress.** Designed and built by my husband, Jeff, it includes straw-bale walls, solar electricity, passive solar heating and cooling, superefficient appliances, natural roofing (living plants and cedar), local nontoxic materials, radiant floor heating, water heated by a wood stove, plenty of daylight, insulated curtains, an indoor greenhouse, and a garden that feeds us for much of the year.

Andrea Burns *lives in Sanbornton, New Hampshire, where she and her husband grow much of their own food and homeschool their kids. She enjoys hiking, swimming, and playing music.*

The Burns homestead in Sanbornton, New Hampshire. Photo by Andrea Burns.

One Professor in a Classroom

Melanie Szulczewski

WHEN YOU HEAR THE SOUND OF SNORING IN YOUR classroom as you discuss the causes and implications of global warming, it is easy to become discouraged. And when a skeptical student asks, "Can one person really make a difference?" sometimes all I can do is sigh and wearily think, *I'm trying to.*

As I observe my students drive to campus in their SUVs and balk at taking the subway for a group trip to a science museum, clamoring instead for the gas-guzzling vans other professors use, I can't help but consider the nature of my role as an environmental science professor. Should I limit myself to explaining the facts behind the greenhouse effect and the consequences to the earth's ecosystems from climate change? Perhaps I shouldn't try to persuade students to become stewards of their environment by showing graphs of carbon-dioxide emissions from various sources and then displaying images of fuel-efficient cars and compact fluorescent light bulbs and the cumulative effects of using them. I even try appealing to their wallets by having them calculate the savings to their electricity bills and fuel-pump expenses if they changed to a more sustainable lifestyle. One student raises his hand to ask, "Will that formula be on the test?" Sigh.

Then, at the end of the semester, a student shows up with a newspaper and a bulging plastic bag. She waves the paper enthusiastically and says, "There's a sale on compact fluorescent light bulbs—I just bought two packs!" Another student asks for directions to the store and explains that she convinced her mother to buy a front-loading washing machine. As the students chatter about their ideas for reducing their carbon footprints and for pass-

> Should I limit myself to **explaining the facts** behind the greenhouse effect...?

ing on information to their families, I realize that they *have* been listening to me. But, more importantly, their new knowledge has motivated many of them to take action to reduce their carbon-dioxide emissions and even persuade others to do so too. I feel rejuvenated as I conclude that no matter what some experts say, one professor in a classroom really can make a difference.

Melanie Szulczewski *is an assistant professor of earth and environmental sciences at the University of Mary Washington in Fredericksburg, Virginia.*

Passing It On

SUMMER 1984, IOWA. My sister and I are stepping carefully through tall, marshy reeds along the shore of Little Spirit Lake. Leopard frogs are tricky to catch, much faster than docile toads. Our mother points out the local creatures in a field guide. I am eight years old, blissfully innocent of the connection between my amphibian friends' survival and the planetary warming caused by my own species' dependence on fossil fuels.

EARTH DAY 1990, IOWA. I am fourteen, proudly wearing a T-shirt admonishing "Cool It!" across a picture of the earth. I am an earnest member of the World Wildlife Fund, which graciously accepts my periodic gifts of five dollars.

JULY 2006, CALIFORNIA. I am admiring a snow bank dripping rhythmically into the glassiest of lakes. My vantage point is a tiny inflatable boat that my husband has packed in for our trek into the Sierra Nevada. We set up camp by Heather Lake, cradled by granite peaks and wind-contorted pines. It occurs to me that this very snow is a vital water source for people all over the state. It feeds lakes, streams, and reservoirs. Yet the Sierra snow pack is already diminishing because of climate change. In a few generations, I wonder, will these mountains be dry?

AUGUST 2007, IOWA. I am five months pregnant and need to make a grocery run. After several years in the hectic San Francisco area, we have returned to our home state, close to family. I think back to the life we fashioned in California, where I biked to work, took the train to Sierra Club meetings, and walked to the farmers' market. At present, it is 95 degrees and oppressively humid. The thought of a thirty-minute walk to the store is too miserable to contemplate, so I get into the car. My low-impact habits will need some adjusting.

SEPTEMBER 2008, IOWA. I am pushing our Sunlawn reel mower across the yard when a neighborhood kid comes over. "Cool!" he says. He has never seen a mower that uses only human power. "Can I try?" Soon the girl across the street wants a turn. Two more kids appear. "My turn!" I laugh at the sight of four young people vying for the chance to mow my lawn pollution-free.

OCTOBER 2008, Iowa. I am on a step stool picking lima beans, the baby watching from a blanket. She shifts her focus to the grass, picks a blade, examines it like a miniature scientist. I'm poised to hop down should she decide to give it the taste test, but I'm happy to let her explore. I was raised to see the value of toads and trees alike; this is a gift I want to pass on. To this ethos I will add the responsibility we all share to protect human life—and indeed all living things—by minimizing our impact on air, water, and climate. Buy less stuff, eat plants, ride your bicycle, clean with vinegar, print on both sides, hang out the laundry. Every choice matters.

> She shifts her focus to the grass, picks a blade, examines it like a **miniature scientist.**

Gillian Zaharias Miller *is a former research engineer who now works as a part-time scientific editor and full-time mom. She lives in rural eastern Iowa with her husband, daughter, and adopted hound.*

Gabriel Filippelli

The Last of the Carnivores

TO STAND ON TOP OF A DUNE RIDGE IN THE INDIANA Dunes National Lakeshore is to straddle the natural and industrial worlds. Several hundred feet to the north is the sandy shoreline of Lake Michigan, one of the Great Lakes, which contain most of the world's fresh water. Upwind to the west is the heart of U.S. steel production, with the smokestacks of Gary and Hammond emitting a gray-black cloud that languidly drifts overhead. Just to the south, between serene dune peaks, is a shallow swale that contains some of the most exotic plants in North America.

Home to a panne ecosystem—an exceedingly rare environment comprising over 1,400 unique plant species—these coastal dune lands along the shores of Lake Michigan were formed thousands of years ago, after the final retreat of the Laurentide ice sheet. Human-caused erosion is evident here, but these dunes are relatively resistant to everything except bulldozers. Unfortunately, the fragile panne ecosystems that they enclose are not so resilient.

It was here that I first introduced my son to that greatest object of fascination for young boys—carnivorous plants! Insect-eating pitcher plants are a characteristic panne species, one my son learned about when studying the ecosystems of Indiana in grade school. Seeing his excitement as he raced down the dunes and knelt, brushing and prodding the pitcher plants to see their response, reminded me of my own fascination with nature, which propelled me into science, and of the power of nature to teach about complexity and interactions and absolute wonder.

Being able to share this wonderful world with my son, while contrails from O'Hare Airport and smoke from

...the power of nature to teach about **complexity and interactions** and absolute wonder.

a nearby steel plant colored the sky, gave me a sense of hope about the world. But this magical place may very well be among the ever-lengthening list of unique environments that vanish from the earth, victims of global climate change and associated changes in temperature and rainfall.

The invasion of these ecosystems by cattails and Egyptian reeds over the past twenty years is what brought me to the dunes in the first place, to solve a puzzle. How did this ecosystem withstand more than one hundred years of industrial pollution, including brutal assaults on the atmosphere before the Clean Air Act, when the skies were regularly clouded by smokestack haze? And now, when the skies are clearer, why did it begin to succumb to invasion by exotics? Could the recent rapid drop in the level of Lake Michigan, due in large part to global climate change, be the cause?

That this fragile and beautiful environment persisted in the face of extreme industrialization gave me hope for the resilience of nature. But the fear that it is rapidly disappearing through the insults of global climate change makes me despair for my children's children, who may never be able to meet this hidden world with its carnivorous plants nestled within rolling sand dunes, just a twenty-five-minute drive east of Chicago.

Gabriel Filippelli *is a professor and chair of the Earth Sciences Department at Indiana University–Purdue University Indianapolis (IUPUI). He lives in Indianapolis with his wife and their three children.*

My Grandson

I want my grandchildren to know I care desperately about the world they will inherit, a world I want them to love as much as I love them. It seems an overwhelming task to curb global warming, but **each day I try to do at least one thing—** writing to an elected official, turning off some lights, walking or biking instead of driving, talking to others—to demonstrate my concern and willingness to change the trajectory we are on.

Kate Crowley *is a naturalist and freelance writer who lives on twenty acres outside of Willow River, Minnesota, with her husband, Mike Link.*

My grandson, Ryan Carlson, in Banning State Park, Minnesota. Photo by Mike Link.

Eating Healthy for the Planet

Una McGeough

LATELY MY EFFORTS TO DO THE RIGHT THING (FOR my kids, for the planet) have focused on food. It started with a cake—a pumpkin spice layer cake. This cake was special, beyond the beaten butter, grated nutmeg, and sifted flour. The extra touch was a homegrown pumpkin. We sowed the seed, tended the plant, harvested the pumpkin; then I gutted, peeled, steamed, and pureed it. That hefty but delicate orange squash was folded into the cake batter and baked, giving new meaning to the concept of cooking from scratch.

I love to cook and to eat good food, but my thoughts about food evolved as I read more about the energy used and pollution generated to bring the basics to my kitchen. I've worked for many years with organizations promoting renewable energy and energy efficiency. I've gaped at the climate-change naysayers and turned my indignation inward: what more can *I* do? I've bought compact fluorescent lights and lowered my thermostat and tuned up my bike. But when I thought about food, the question of how to feed my family a nutritious, tasty, economical diet that is good for the planet seemed very complicated.

So we planted a plot in the community garden with room for sprawling pumpkin and watermelon vines. While we harvested lettuce, cucumbers, peas, carrots, basil, and flowers, we marveled at our food: fresh, tasty, homegrown. The new vogue for "healthy-for-the-planet eating" is actually old-fashioned. It's the small farm, the kitchen garden, the local dairy. In many places, local has never gone out of style.

In many places, **local has never gone** out of style.

Locally grown food isn't shipped thousands of miles, gulping oil, generating pollution, and consuming more than its own caloric value to reach your dinner table. Food grown yourself or by a farmer nearby can be picked when it's ripest and most flavorful. Think global (warming), act (buy) local (food).

So I try to do the right thing without supporting the long-distance food system, which is the norm. Instead of produce from around the world, I choose Michigan's fruit whenever possible. When you live in metro Chicago, that's pretty local. Our aging apple tree yielded a bumper crop this year—what could be more local than pies and applesauce from our back yard? And going to the farmers' market is a favorite way to spend Sunday mornings.

That pumpkin cake tasted of possibility. At a time when the path to the dinner table is strewn with contamination hazards and prohibitions, from trans fats to tuna, farmed salmon to French toast, there is joy in the abundance of a farmers' market or your own back yard. Turning the tide on global warming might be more palatable than you think.

As far as doing the right thing for my kids, I'm not sure where local food fits in with regular bedtimes and good schools. But I've become convinced that it *is* part of doing the right thing for the planet, and what could be better for my kids than that?

Una McGeough *worked as a small business contractor for the Environmental Protection Agency in North Carolina and led a renewable energy development nonprofit in Ohio. She lives in Skokie, Illinois, with her husband and three sons.*

Rick Lindroth

Man Freezes Out Family

Preach the Gospel at all times. If necessary, use words.
—*attributed to St. Francis of Assisi*

HANGING ABOVE OUR THERMOSTAT IS A NONE-TOO- flattering photograph of me—hair disheveled, eyes downcast as if I'm being led off to prison—with a headline from our local newspaper: "Man Freezes Out Family for No Reason." It was a gift... from my children.

Those who enter our home during winter are quick to appreciate the humor. In our household, caring for the earth has priority over many personal comforts. This value has not always been held by every family member. My wife had a choice early on: marry me or someone else. My two daughters, however, had no choice. Which brings me to the point of this essay.

Educational psychologists tell us that people behave according to what they *believe* rather than what they *know*. Changing our behavior requires changing our beliefs. Otherwise, I fear, there is little hope for resolving our climate crisis.

As an ecologist, I speak about the dangers of climate change to school classes, faith-based groups, legislators, and the general public. Although I try to make a compelling case for environmental responsibility, I am not naive about the success of my efforts. Climate-change naysayers, still surprisingly abundant, are rarely swayed. Why? In general, it's not that they need more facts. What they need is a change of mind—preceded by a change of heart.

Modeling and *experience* are powerful tools for shaping values and, thus, behaviors. For nearly two decades we modeled for our daughters a lifestyle shaped by concern for the environment: we converted a fifty-year-old house to be energy efficient, commuted to work by bicycle (even during Wisconsin winters), bought energy-efficient appliances, paid a surcharge for wind-generated electricity, planted trees, composted kitchen waste, and, perhaps

Kawnipi Lake, deep within Quetico Provincial Park in Canada, is one of my favorite canoeing destinations. Photo by Rick Lindroth.

most noticeable to adolescent daughters, refused to capitulate to a culture of consumption.

We also engaged them in the wonder and challenges of the natural world. While their friends jetted to luxurious vacation destinations, we camped our way around Lake Superior and canoed in the boreal wilderness of Quetico Provincial Park. While their friends experienced the faux summer of indoor water parks, we went winter-camping. All those years I had doubts as to our daughters' own environmental ethics: the house was always too hot or too cold; recycling was too difficult.

I no longer hold those doubts. Since leaving home, my daughters have become environmental missionaries, setting the pace for roommates and friends. Some of their environmentally conscious practices go beyond my own; they now challenge me.

My wife and I still strive to convince others of the critical need to make lifestyle changes. But we now recognize that our greatest impact comes not from what we say but from our modeling of a consistent earth ethic.

Recently my younger daughter visited us, roommate and bags of compost in tow. Seeing a programmable thermostat on our kitchen table, her roommate quipped: "What happened, did your old thermostat freeze and break?" We laughed. And I smiled: little does she know how her life is about to change.

Rick Lindroth *is a professor of ecology at the University of Wisconsin—Madison. He studies the impacts of global environmental change on northern forest ecosystems.*

Acknowledgments

I WAS ON THE ROAD TO ATLANTA WITH MY WIFE
over the holidays, reading one of the nearly one thousand submissions we received for this anthology—she was driving—when I turned to her and said that with another editor or another team of reviewers, this book might look completely different. We received so many strong contributions that narrowing the field proved extremely difficult. Every voice speaking out on climate change should be heard.

With that in mind, I want to begin this effusive outpouring by thanking the talented and committed individuals who wrote and submitted essays and contributed photographs for *Thoreau's Legacy*. Thank you for taking the time to create these accounts and share your lives with us. To the selected authors, an extra word of appreciation for all your patience in what must have seemed an interminable production schedule. You are a great group of people, and I've enjoyed getting to know you.

At the Union of Concerned Scientists, this project received quick and enthusiastic backing from our leadership, in particular Kevin Knobloch, Kathy Rest, Lance Pierce, Peter Frumhoff, and the person who was always there to listen and guide, Suzanne Shaw. The talented team that helped get the word out to the public included Karla Capers, Nancy Cole, Kate Abend, Meredith Rutrick, Katy Love, and Rouwenna Lamm. Jean Sideris was a captain of this crew and also a key reviewer of essays. Colleen MacDonald made important contributions at all stages, as did the entire UCS communications department. Brenda Ekwurzel read each essay with a discerning scientific eye, even when she didn't have time. And Brian Halley was an invaluable resource in reviewing essays and offering advice on all things "book."

It has been a pleasure to work with our partners and new friends at Penguin Classics. John Fagan, the man who helped engineer it all, was there from the conception of the project to review of the essays to the rollout of the book. John, I couldn't have asked for a better partner. The leadership of Kathryn Court and Elda Rotor was vital to the success of the anthology. Maureen Donnelly helped get *Thoreau's Legacy* on track and coordinated publicity along with Gabrielle Gantz. Molly Barton at Penguin Group judged essays and helped narrow the field of entries. Thanks also to Dennis Swaim and Lynn Rogan of the advertising and promotion team; Jeff Gomez and Kristin O'Connell of Penguin Online; Bibi Baksh in marketing; and Norm Lidofsky, Trish Weyenberg, Patrick Nolan, and the entire Penguin Group paperback sales force. The fabulous Sabrina Bowers designed the hardback version of the book.

Support for this project extends beyond UCS and Penguin Classics. Aric Caplan made a very productive connection that helped launch this partnership, and Cynthia Schumm and Benjamin Smith at Bright Satellite provided important advice and promotional support. Our appreciation goes to the hundreds of booksellers who displayed *Thoreau's Legacy* easels in their stores. We are grateful to Barbara Kingsolver for contributing her foreword during a very busy time, as well as to Judy Carmichael for her help. And one large bear hug to Meghan Hayes, who never complained when the anthology's editor spent many late nights at the computer.

I am indebted to Peg Anderson, our first-class manuscript editor and an unsung hero of the anthology. Peg, you wield a precise and caring editing pen. Finally, to Sheryl Eisenberg and Lori Gomes, the creative maestros at Mixit Productions: you somehow read my mind every step of the way. Thanks to both of you for bringing the authors' hard work to life. It's been a privilege.

—Richard Hayes